The College & Career Companion

Navigating the CAO System in Ireland

By Seamus Whitney & Mary Hickey

Version1.0 – January 2025

Website: https://www.whitneycareerguidance.com
Website: https://maryhickeycareerguidance.com

Published by: Mary Hickey and Seamus Whitney

ISBN: 978-1-0369-1254-3

Cover Design and Internal Design: By Barry O' Sullivan Artist.

Contents

Introduction

"The more I research, the more confused I become."

Does the above quote sound familiar to you? If you're feeling lost or unsure about which career path to take, you're not alone. So many people are saying to us how difficult it has become to navigate their way around careers information. Even though we now have more information than ever before, the net result is that people are more confused than ever. Navigating the world of college and careers can be overwhelming. However, there is help at hand, and this is the main reason we wrote this book.

For over twenty-five years we have been helping people sort through the maze of careers information. It is amazing to see the amount of misinformation that is out there. There is a myriad of courses that make bold promises about career and employment prospects. Students are often lured onto courses with expectations of concrete results, only to discover that the information provided was, well, 'not quite accurate', in the first instance. Our focus has always been to cut through the layers of unending data and provide students with a methodology that helps them find the information they need. Armed with this accurate knowledge, they are then able to make more informed decisions regarding their future.

So, what do we do about all of this?

Over the years the focus of our career assessments has always been work. Rightly or wrongly, we firstly set out to identify where each candidate would see themselves working, and what kind of role they would be performing. Potential salaries also play a major role in this decision-making process. For us it is very important for students (and their parents) that upon graduation from their course or apprenticeship, they have a good chance of gaining meaningful employment in a job that pays a wage that is reliable and leads to a sustainable lifestyle

How to use this book:

This book is your roadmap to finding a career that not only aligns with your skills and passions, but also brings you lasting fulfilment. We'll explore practical strategies, proven techniques, and insightful reflections to help you make informed and inspired career choices.

We have broken down the career areas **into 17 broad sections**, and these sectors are listed in the contents page. For ease of navigation, you should review the contents carefully in advance. Start with those areas of employment that have a strong appeal for you. Then refer to the chapter in question as laid out in the contents page and follow the course recommendations that we give you. We have set out to give you the benefit of our experience in this regard. This methodology is extended throughout all the chapters. Spending time reviewing these will save you endless time and should also avoid the possibility of you 'falling into the information abyss'.

Your career is not just a means to an end; it's a journey of self-discovery, growth, and contribution. By the time you finish this book, you'll have the clarity and confidence to pursue a career that excites you and aligns with your true self.

How will I know what career suits me best?

Of course, this is a core question that many students have. How will they be sure that this is the right area for them. Within each chapter we have attempted to address this, by referring to what we feel are the key issues that aspiring students face when considering a particular career path. We also refer to the key personal characteristics that we think are very important for people to become successful in each of the individual career sectors. This is based on assessing thousands of people over a long period of time, and receiving feedback from them on how their course and career progressed. There is no cast iron method for guaranteeing absolute success in pinpointing the 'right career' for a young person. Students in their late teens are still changing and developing, and they must be allowed space to find what it is they love doing in their own unique way of engaging with the world.

As Career Guidance Advisors we do have vast experience of helping people identify what they are most suitable for. With over twenty-five years of experience in career counselling and having guided thousands of individuals to their ideal careers, we've seen first-hand what it takes to turn dreams into reality. Over the years we have developed a series of preference and aptitude tests which help pinpoint a student's strengths and interests. Because of the complexity of carrying out individual assessments, we can't offer this advice through this book. However, if you would like to avail of an assessment tailored to your needs, you can contact us through our website,

www.whitneycareerguidance.com

www.maryhickeycareerguidance.com

With the advent of modern technology, we can offer you an assessment regardless of where you are based in the country.

As you turn the pages, we encourage you to reflect deeply, take notes, and most importantly, act on the insights you discover. This is your opportunity to take control of your future and create a career that not only meets your needs but also fulfils your deepest aspirations.

Chapter One

Early Years and Primary Teaching

The teaching archetype attracts confident people with good people skills. In this instance, we think of adult trainers, conference presenters and sports coaches. The challenge of effective teaching is always one of helping each student get a grasp of the fundamental concepts they need to understand. The best teachers are able to identify the specific needs of each learner and communicate with them on that level.

Some students seem to be born with teaching as a vocation. One of the most common things we have heard over the years is something like:

> **"All she/he ever wanted from a young age was to be a primary teacher."**

The profession of teaching does not just cover school teachers. Any profession that requires clear explanation of concepts and ideas can be considered a teaching profession.

However for the purpose of this book, in this section, we will cover careers in Early Years Education, Montessori, Primary Teaching and Post Primary Teaching.

Early Years Education:

Early Years Educators work with children at the foundation stage of learning and they traditionally are found working in crèches and playschools. The age of these children can span anywhere from four months to five years and the role of the early years educator will be determined by the age of their charges. For example, one teacher could be working in the baby room ensuring all physical needs of the baby are addressed, while another might be in the toddler or pre-school room where there is more of an emphasis on learning through play. Regardless of the age group, elevated levels of energy and acute observational skills are paramount in this role.

Entry level requirements to work in this area start with a QQI Level 5 Award normally achieved by completing a Post Leaving Certificate Course (PLC) in Childcare or Early Childhood Care and Education. These courses are available nationwide in Colleges of Further Education.

Possessing an Honours Degree in Early Childhood Education will increase opportunities for career progression, for example in roles such as Room Leader or Childcare Manager.

A degree in Early Childhood Education is often used as a pathway into post graduate primary school teaching (see Primary Teaching). There are a number of degree options available including but not limited to:

BA Early Childhood Teaching and Learning (fulltime) at **Maynooth University (MH003)** and a flexible learning pathway **(MH004).**

BA Early Childhood Education TUD Grangegorman (TU995).

BA of Early Childhood Education at DCU (DC001).

BA Early Years and Childhood Studies at UCC (CK111).

BA In Early Childhood Care and Education at Mary Immaculate Limerick (MI007).

BA Early Childcare and Education at SETU Waterford (SE911), Carlow (SE913) and Wexford (SE912).

BA Early Childhood Education & Care at TUS Athlone (US926).

Monstessori Teaching:

While there is often a lot of crossover between the role of the Early Years Educator and that of a Montessori Teacher, the main difference is that the Montessori Teacher places more of an emphasis on academic learning via play. Students in the Montessori school learn about the world the environment, cultures, languages and maths.

Private colleges including **St. Nicholas College, Dun Laoghaire** (CAO Application) and **Portobello Institute in Dublin** (Direct Application) both provide qualifications in Montessori Teaching. Prospective students need to research these colleges in more detail, paying particular attention to the fees which tend to be higher than fees in the public colleges. Students who are applying for a SUSI Grant need to be aware that these colleges **are not covered under the SUSI scheme.**

Munster Technological University Cork Campus offer a BA Honours Degree in Montessori Teaching via the CAO **(MT970)**.

> **Tip:** Studying Home Economics at Leaving Certificate is helpfulfor students considering a career in the Early Years and Montessori Sectors.

Primary Teaching:

Interest in primary teaching remains steady year on year. This interest can stem from students own experience of primary school, an inspirational teacher, or having family members working as primary teachers. The role of a primary teacher is quite broad and involves a lot of multi-tasking. Duties can include nurturing the child, developing their literacy and numerical skills, involving parents in the educational journey, while teaching all subjects on the ever-changing curriculum. Lesson planning, reflection on teaching techniques, managing challenging behaviours, working with children with special educational needs, and ensuring a safe and constructive teaching environment are all important parts of this very important education role.

Regardless of the influencing factors, students considering primary teaching need to enter the career fully informed and for the correct reasons.

There are various options available to qualify in primary teaching with the four-year Bachelor of Education (B.Ed.) being the most straightforward.

Entry into the Bachelor of Education is competitive and generally requires high points in the region of 475 +. Entry also requires minimum grades in Irish at H4 (60 to 69%), and Maths and English at O4 or H7.

The Bachelor of Education Degree is available at:

DCU: St. Pats Campus, (DC002 & also DC004*)
*Additional Eligibility Criteria applies.

Maynooth University: Froebel College (MH001).

Marino Institute of Education, Dublin (CM001).

Marino Institute of Education, Dublin (CM003). Oideachas Bunmhuinteoireacht Tri Mhean na Gaeilge). Please note that a H3 (70 to 79%) in Irish is required in addition to sitting Teastas Eorpach na Gaeilge (TEG) Meánleibhéal 1 (B1) examination. Students can gain up to a maximum of forty additional points towards this course depending on their grade in the B1 examination.

Mary Immaculate College Limerick (MI005).

Mary Immaculate College offer variations on their B.Ed. These primary teaching degrees include the B.Ed. International **(MI004),** and the B.Ed. Psychology **(MI008).** These two courses attract many applicants and points tend to be higher than the B.Ed courses with points averaging around the mid to high 500's.

Post Graduate Studies in Primary Teaching

For students who wish to or need to access primary teaching via **post graduate study** they will commence their journey by completing a honours degree in their chosen discipline. There is no specific primary degree requirement but common options include: early year's education, social sciences, arts, humanities, and social care. However, students have progressed to primary teaching from primary degrees in many other disciplines.

Post Graduate Study options are available in Ireland and the UK. For those applying for the Professional (PME) **in Ireland,** minimum Leaving Certificate grades apply including, Irish at H4 (60 to 69%), and Maths and English at O4/H7. It is advised that students always check these requirements with the provider as they are open to change. The PME is two years in duration and can be studied through two learning methods including:

Full time class room learning with **DCU, Maynooth, Marino Institute** of Education and **Mary Immaculate College.** Candidates wishing to apply for this option must sit the Teastas Eorpach Gaeilge (TEG) Level B1 Oral Irish examination. A minimum of 65% must be attained.

The Blended Learning option with **Hibernia College** involves self-directed learning, lectures online, and attendance at face-to-face classes throughout the duration of the PME. It is recommended that students should allocate 37 hours weekly to their studies. The application process includes a competitive interview with a minimum of ten minutes conducted through the medium of Irish and thirty minutes facilitated via English.

For those wishing to qualify via post graduate study in the **UK** there is an extensive range of choices available. Among those more popular options are Northern Ireland via **Ulster University** or **Queens University** through the Medium of Irish. In the UK Irish students have been successful at **John Moore's University in Liverpool, Edge Hill University in Ormskirk, St. Marys University in Twickenham** and **Swansea University in Wales.** All of the above institutions offer a Post Graduate Certificate in Primary Education (PGCE). The PGCE can be 1 or 2 years in duration depending on where you study. In Scotland, **University of Edinburgh** and **Dundee University** offer the Post Graduate Diploma in Education Primary (PGDE) over 2 years. Colleges in the UK will expect students to have qualifying Leaving Certificate Grades in Maths, English and a Science Subject (Biology, Chemistry or Physics) in order to meet necessary entry criteria.

Some students will make the decision to complete their four year undergraduate teacher training in the UK. This involves making a UCAS application. While a big part of this application is based on the student's personal statement, they must also present with minimum subject grades in the Leaving Certificate including; Maths, English and a Science Subject (Biology, Chemistry or Physics) in order to meet necessary entry criteria.

*__Students returning from the UK__ (from both undergraduate training or post graduate training) will need to get their teaching qualification recognised and register with the Teaching Council of Ireland. This will involve the completion of a Department of Education Irish Course and Exam for example: an aptitude test (Scrúdú le hAghaidh Cáilíochta sa Ghaeilge – SCG) or an adaption period (Oiriúnú le hAghaidh Cáilíochta sa Ghaeilge – OCG). Students have a three year period from when they return to Ireland to complete this process. Returning graduates may teach during this period normally subbing, maternity leave cover etc. Students qualifying in the UK are now often finding themselves having to complete some courses in history and religion in order to satisfy the needs of the Teaching Council of Ireland.

Tip 1: If applying to the UK please make sure you apply for the PGCE / PGDE to teach the age group 3 to 12 or 5 to 12 years.

Tip 2: Regardless of where you apply to for post graduate study the best guidance is to get as much experience as you can in a classroom environment. This is essential if applying to NI or the UK.

Chapter Two

Post Primary Teaching

Post Primary Teaching:

If you wish to educate young people, cultivate their interest and passion in **specific subjects**, foster their independence and prepare them for life after school, post primary teaching could be the area for you. Post primary teachers must be positive role models, they must be able to connect with young people at an appropriate level and engage in a mutually beneficial and respectful alliance. Post primary teachers will normally teach two subjects in various combinations, and there are a large range of subjects to choose from. Strong employment opportunities exist particularly in the areas of language teaching (including Irish), Science and Mathematics. Other subjects that also are experiencing strong demand include Home Economics and technical subjects such as Design and Communication Graphics (DCG). While teachers of other subjects may initially find it challenging to gain full time employment, our advice is to be patient until opportunities arise.

Physical Education Teaching:

Physical Education remains a popular choice with students, but entry points are quite high due to the demand among our sports mad student population. Courses are generally four-year Honours Degrees, and Graduates are fully qualified to teach Physical Education plus their chosen choice subject. There is no need to complete a PME as teaching practice is an integral part of the Degree course. These courses comprise of in depth study of Physical Education modules, the choice subject and education modules, including lesson planning, the Leaving Certificate Physical Education curriculum, teaching methods, and time spent in the classroom as a trainee teacher. The following courses are available:

University of Limerick (LM090): This is the longest established course. Physical Education can be combined with Geography, Maths, Irish, English and Drama.
University College Cork (CK125): This course combines Physical Education with English, Irish, Maths, French or History. A Third language is an entry requirement for this programme.
Dublin City University has two options:
DC205 with Biology requires O4/H6 in Maths.
DC206 with Maths requires O1/H6 in Maths.
Applicants will need a laboratory science subject at O4 or H6 level as an entry requirement for both these courses at DCU.

There are alternative options to qualify as a Physical Education Teacher, including the completion of a Primary Degree, for example, Coaching Science & Sports Pedagogy at **MTU Cork** or BSc Hons in Physical Education & Coaching at **Portobello College** - plus the completion of a P.M.Ed. at the **University of Limerick.** These pathways qualify graduates to teach Physical Education only and this can be a disadvantage when applying for teaching positions.

For already qualified post primary teachers who are registered with the Teaching Council of Ireland, there are also options to add Physical Education to their existing subject specialties. This can be achieved by completing a specific Higher Diploma in Physical Education at **MTU Tralee** or **Portobello College** in Dublin over a part time basis.

Science Teaching:

Those aspiring to qualify as Science Teachers have two routes to qualification.

Route A.

Complete a Specific Science Education Degree. These B.Ed.'s are designed to qualify you as a Science Teacher in Biology / Chemistry / Physics / Agricultural Science / Mathematics in specific combinations. There is no need to complete a PME following completion of these courses as Teaching Practice is an integral part of these courses. There are various options available.

University of Limerick offers a four-year Level 8 BSc concurrent Science Education pathway.

BSc Science Education Biology with Chemistry OR Physics OR Ag Science **(LM092)**.

BSc Mathematics and Computer Science Education **(LM097)**.

BSc Physics and Chemistry Education **(LM096)**.

DCU (DC203) lists a four-year Level 8 BSc. Concurrent Science Education degree in Chemistry, Physics, Maths. (choose 2 in year 3).

UCC (CK413) provides a four-year Level 8 BSc Concurrent Science Education with options in; Biology and Chemistry, Physics and Maths, Computer Science and Maths, Chemistry and Maths, Computer Science and Chemistry.

UCD offers a five-year Master of Education at Level 9 via their Common Entry Science Degree (DN200) with options to combine Maths and Applied Maths, Maths and Biology, Maths and Chemistry and Maths and Physics.

Maynooth University also provide a five-year Master of Education at Level 9 including options in: Biology, Chemistry, Physics, Maths. (Choose two after first year) **(MH212SED)**. Mathematics and Computer Science **(MH212MCS),** or Maths & Applied Maths **(MH212MED)**.

Route B.

Alternatively students can qualify by completing a Level 8 Honours Degree in Science (BSc Hons). For example: Biological and Biomedical Sciences at **NUIM**, General Science at **UCD,** Biological or Pharmaceutical Science at **SETU** and then complete a two-year PME Post Primary and teach the Science Discipline(s) covered in their Degree.

Agricultural Science Teaching:

To qualify as a teacher of Agricultural Science, students can complete the Science Education degree in **UL** which has an Agricultural Science option in combination with Biology **(LM092)**, normally around 500 points.

Alternatively students can complete a four-year Agricultural Science Degree at **UCD** or **SETU Waterford** for example, and then complete a two-year PME to qualify as an Agricultural Science Teacher. These Agricultural Science Degrees have been averaging around the 400 mark for the last two years.

Maths Teaching:

Students wishing to pursue Maths teaching can avail of the above mentioned relevant options or consider,
University of Galway's four-year option BA Maths Education (GY109).

Mary Immaculate College Thurles Campus: Four-year options: in Maths with Irish **(MI013)** or Maths with Business **(MI014)**.

Alternatively students can complete a Maths related Degree. For example: Mathematical Science in **UCC (CK407)** or Maths via Arts (combine with another subject) at any of the country's major Universities and then add the two-year PME Post Primary.

Language Teaching:

Teaching languages is an option to consider for those gifted with a strong ability in these increasingly important subjects. Students can complete a four-year Bachelor of Education in the languages of their choice with course options available at:

DCU: Study Irish with one of French, German or Spanish, (DC013).

Applicants must present with a minimum of H3 in their two choice languages.

UCC: Irish with one of the following: French, Spanish, German, or Italian, **(CK124).** A H3 is required in Irish and French where as a H4 is sufficient in German, Spanish and Italian.

UCD: Students can choose between studying two languages from French, Spanish, German, Italian and/or Irish or choose Irish on its own (B.Ed. in Gaeilge) **(DN760).** Students must present with a minimum of H5 in Irish and a minimum of H4 in one or more modern language depending on the combined languages.

UL: Choose two languages from French, German, Japanese and Spanish **(LM091).** You will need to hold a Leaving Certificate grade of a H3 in one of the two languages.

Alternatively students can complete a L8 Honours Degree with Languages, for example: World Languages, Modern Languages, European Languages, and Languages via Arts, and then add a two-year PME Post Primary to qualify.

Design Communication and Graphics, Woodwork, Metalwork, Technical Graphics, Technology and Construction Teaching:

Students who excel at the practical subjects such as Woodwork, Tech Graph and Engineering often show an interest in teaching these subjects at post primary level.

University of Limerick has a long tradition of qualifying teachers of all the main practical subjects. Their two main degrees **(LM094 & LM095)** have been to the forefront for over twenty-five years. The points requirements are generally in the 450-500 region for **(LM094)** and a little lower at 400-450 for **(LM095).**

Bachelor of Technology in Graphics & Construction Technology, **(LM094)** upon graduation you can teach Woodwork, Tech Graph and Technology to Junior Certificate level and Construction Studies and DCG to Leaving Certificate level.

BTech Materials and Engineering Technology, **(LM095)** upon graduation you can teach Metalwork, Technology and Tech Graph to Junior Certificate level and Engineering, Technology and DCG to Leaving Certificate level.

ATU Galway is another major provider and has two options.

(AU680): Upon graduation you can teach Woodwork, Tech Graph and Technology to Junior Certificate level and Construction Studies and DCG to Leaving Certificate level. Years 1 and 2 are spent at the ATU Connemara Campus in Letterfrack.

(AU620): Allows students to teach Art and Technical Graphics to Junior Certificate level and Art and DCG to Leaving Certificate level.

DCU/TUS Athlone (DC015) is a relatively new addition, and graduates are qualified to teach Metalwork, Technology and Tech Graph to Junior Certificate level and Engineering, Technology and DCG to Leaving Certificate level. The first two-years of this course are spent at TUS Athlone, and years three and four are spent at DCU.

For the student who wishes to teach Construction Studies only, a good option is Building Surveying at **Dundalk (DK830)** plus a two year PME Post Primary at **UL**.

Home Economics Teaching:

For many years **St. Angela's in Sligo (now ATU)** was the only option to study Home Economics Teaching in Ireland. New providers have come on board in recent years and these new courses have opened up more opportunities for those interested in teaching this popular subject. Students now have the opportunity to study Home Economics in Thurles, County Tipperary at the **Mary Immaculate Campus** or at **MTU/UCC** in Cork, which is a joint programme. These new courses combine Home Economics with Business Studies. Students also have the option to combine Home Economics with Technology on the joint programme between TUS Athlone and DCU.

Demand for places has been high with course places being offered only to those applicants who reach a minimum of 450 points rising to 500 points and beyond. ATU Sligo (St. Angela's) campus allows students to qualify to teach Home Economics plus one other subject within a four-year period.

Course options: Home Economics and Biology **(AU985),** Religion **(AU986),** Irish, **(AU987)** or choose Home Economics as a single subject (AU988).

MTU Cork and **UCC:** This combined college option offers a five-year qualification to teach Home Economics and Business **(MT930).** Mary Immaculate Thurles provide a four-year qualification to teach Home Economics and Business **(MI022).**

TUS Athlone and DCU: This joint course allows students to qualify to teach Home Economics with Technology over four years **(DC016)**

An alternative route to qualifying is offered at **St. Angela's** where students can study a four-year BA Home Economics at **ATU (AU990)** before progressing on to the two-year PME Post Primary.

Business Teaching:

There are a number of options available to qualify as a Business Teacher.

Mary Immaculate Thurles offer a four-year concurrent qualification to teach business alongside a combination of different subjects including Accounting **(MI016)**, Religion **(MI017)**, Irish **(MI019)**, Maths **(MI021)** and Home Economics **(MI022)**.

Graduates will teach Business and their chosen subject to both Junior Certificate and Leaving Certificate level. Points traditionally come in at the 400-450 range.

Alternatively students can choose to complete a Bachelor of Business Studies/ Bachelor of Commerce and then complete the two-year PME Post Primary. The choice of your major options within your Degree may determine what subjects and to what level you will teach at within the post primary sector.

Students may also choose to study Business or Economics combined with another subject within an Arts Degree programme (See BA Degrees). For example a popular option might be combining Business and Geography. Once the student completes the PME Post Primary they can teach their Business subject alongside their second Arts Subject.

Music Teaching:

For those wishing to pursue a career in Music Teaching the most direct route is to apply to **Trinity College** to study the four-year Music Education Degree, **(TR009).** This is a competitive course to gain entry onto as it has an audition and interview as part of the application process. Students applying here will normally have a background in music, either as part of the Leaving Certificate or perhaps studying music as an extra curriculum activity, for example taking piano grades at intermediate or advanced level.

Alternatively students can study one of the many Music Degree options available, including, but not limited to, **MTU Cork, SETU Waterford, Trinity College, TUD's** BIMM and add on the PME Post Primary to qualify to teach music.

Another useful option is to combine Music with another subject within a BA Arts Degree programme for example at **Maynooth, Trinity,** or **UCC** and then adding on the two-year PME Post Primary.

Students should check the entry requirements for all Music Degrees as auditions and interviews are sometimes necessary. In some cases especially for the BA programmes, colleges require Leaving Certificate students to present with Higher Level Music at minimum Grade of H5 or H4.

Some Music Teachers will provide private music lessons outside of the classroom. We should note that there is no one qualification that is standard for those wishing to provide these private lessons. However, having some form of background in music pedagogy is a good idea. **The Royal Irish Academy of Music** (RIAM) and **Comhaltas Ceoltóirí Éireann** provide workshops and training in this area. It is also common place to have studied musical instrument(s) to an advanced grade and to have completed Royal Irish Academy of Music exams.

Art Teaching:

Those creative students studying art at Leaving Certificate often consider teaching Art as opposed to following careers as an artist. The options to qualify include a four-year Education Degree with **NCAD, TUS** or **ATU Galway**. These options are inclusive of teaching practice and carry the full teaching qualification. Entry to these courses requires the presentation of an extensive portfolio of work. Students can gain a number of CAO points towards their college place based on their portfolio of work. It is advised to seek assistance with this portfolio either via a private tutor, an art teacher or through the completion of a QQI Level 5 PLC with the emphasis on portfolio preparation. Here is a breakdown of the courses and relevant entry requirements.

Note: A portfolio, interview and/or skills test is normally part of the application process for entry into any of the General Degrees in Fine Art or Design.

NCAD (AD202): Entry is based on Portfolio only, plus Leaving Certificate Subjects; Irish, English, Maths, plus one of: Third Language/Art/DCG.

TUS (US801): (Joint Program with **TUS & UL**) Entry requirements include the combination of Leaving Certificate results and Portfolio Assessment.

ATU (AU620): Teach Art with DCG. (H5 in one of the Leaving Certificate subjects of Art and DCG is required).

Alternatively students can study a General Degree in Fine Art or Design and progress onto the two-year PME in Art Education available at **NCAD / TUS / MTU** (Crawford College of Art).

Bachelor of Arts (Arts) Degree:

The Arts Degree pathway into post primary school teaching allows students to combine their favourite subjects into a teaching qualification once they have completed the two year PME Post Primary. There is a vast selection of subjects to study via Arts Degrees. We should point out at this stage that Arts Degrees are not exclusively designed to qualify graduates for teaching positions only. While Arts degrees are often a pre cursor to further Post-Graduate studies, there are many and varied outlets depending on the subject combinations.

All of the major Universities in Ireland offer students the option of studying Arts. These include **UCD, UCC, Galway University** and **Maynooth University,** all of which require a third language as a basic entry requirement. T**rinity College, University of Limerick, Mary Immaculate,** and **DCU**, also have excellent options available and these do not require the third language. Some of the Technological Universities also offer Arts as a Degree but subject choices can be more limited.

From year-two of their BA, students can choose between studying a Joint Honours Degree, (Double Major), or a Single Honours Degree, (Major / Minor). For teaching careers the choice of which of these pathways you choose will determine the level you will teach you're subject(s) at. Those with a Joint Honours Degree (Double Major), will be in a position to teach both subjects to Leaving Certificate Level and those with a Single Honours Degree (Major / Minor) will normally teach the major subject to Leaving Certificate Level and the minor subject to Junior Certificate Level.

Arts and Humanities Degrees range from three to four years in duration, with some students deciding to complete an international year through the Erasmus programme. The Arts Degrees at **UL, Mary Immaculate** and **Trinity College** are four-years in duration regardless of a year abroad or not.

Tip: Any student considering entering post primary teaching of any subject through the PME route should consult with The Teaching Council of Ireland to ensure that their Undergraduate Degree meets the specific subject requirements.

The Teaching Archetype:

The note taker, the planner and chief organiser are individuals suited to a career in teaching. Those with multitasking ability, strong and confident communication skills and a passion to educate, not only academically but holistically, align with the attributes needed to thrive in teaching. These individuals want to help others and work with people in a meaningful way. They want to contribute to society and help others to make their mark on society. While their patience can be tested it takes effort to do this. These people can remain calm and portray this while keeping those in their charge in check. They are not only people smart but self-smart and know their limits and boundaries. Assertiveness and ability to explain the most complex subject depending on the cohort of audience is essential. Confidence and positive body language and stature are important. These teacher types can be viewed as inspirational, role models, with a creative and an enthusiastic mind-set. Kindness and a deep interest and attachment to young people is essential, without this you shouldn't even consider teaching.

Good teachers need to be emotionally strong. While we all know about the attractive holidays etc., many don't witness the stress associated with being a teacher in modern day Ireland. For some who are not equipped with the right blend of emotional intelligence, teaching can be a very difficult and pressurised occupation.

Chapter Three:

Healthcare

Healthcare is one of the career areas that we are asked most questions about. There is huge interest in this area among Irish students. This is probably the main reason that points for healthcare college courses are normally very high. Because of the high entry requirements in Ireland, many students apply to study healthcare across Europe and the U.K. Careers in healthcare require a diverse set of skills and qualities, making them suitable for people with specific traits and interests. Here's a breakdown of the types of people who we feel are best suited for healthcare careers:

1. Compassionate and Empathetic

Healthcare professionals frequently interact with patients who are vulnerable, fearful, or in pain. Compassion and empathy allow them to provide comfort and emotional support.

2. Detail-Oriented

Accuracy is crucial in healthcare, whether it's diagnosing a condition, administering medication, or recording patient information. A small mistake can have significant consequences.

3. Good Communication Skills

Clear communication is vital for explaining diagnoses, treatment options, and procedures to patients and their families. It's also essential for collaborating with other healthcare professionals. Because of this being able to work well with others is essential.

4. Resilient and Emotionally Stable

Healthcare can be emotionally taxing, with exposure to trauma, death, and suffering. Professionals need to manage their own emotions while providing care.

5. Strong Work Ethic and Commitment

Healthcare often involves long hours, shift work, and the need to be on call. A strong work ethic and dedication to patient care are essential. Mental and physical robustness is also needed to handle the demands of the healthcare careers.

6. Lifelong Learners

The healthcare field is constantly evolving with new research, technologies, and treatments. Professionals must continually update their knowledge and skills.

7. Ethically Driven

Healthcare professionals must adhere to strict ethical standards, balancing patient care, privacy, and professional integrity.

People who possess a combination of these traits and are motivated by a desire to help others often find fulfilling careers in healthcare. We often meet students who have experienced some type of therapeutic care themselves or perhaps have witnessed a family member avail of such care. In some cases, this experience deepens their interest and their desire to work within the health care field.

Healthcare careers are diverse and for the purpose of this book we have divided them into five broad categories. These sections are as follows:

- **Medicine**
- Careers in **Nursing.**
- Biology based Health Care Careers such as **Physiotherapy.**
- Chemistry based Health Care Careers including **Pharmacy** and **Dentistry.**
- Health Care Careers such as **Radiography** that have a high focus on the use of Technology.

Medicine:

Of all the careers we advise on, Medicine is definitely the most prestigious. Many of the high achieving academic students that attend our practice show an interest in Medicine as a career. It is common even for those that do not show interest in general Healthcare careers to often buck the trend and want to explore Medicine.

Students put great effort into their dream of becoming a doctor. It is a long and sometimes frustrating journey for the young person. This challenging journey begins when they are picking their Leaving Certificate Subjects and continues right through until they qualify.

Becoming a Doctor:

Entry into any of the five colleges offering Medicine at Undergraduate Level is through the **CAO** system. Entry requirements are without question the most competitive in the state, and entry points are a combination of points scored at the Leaving Certificate and points scored at the **HPAT Exams.** *(See Table 1 showing all options to study medicine in Ireland including entry requirements).*

Table 1. The Five Colleges Offering Medicine at Undergraduate Level

College & Code:	Duration : Years:	Science Requirement:	Third Language Requirement :
Trinity (TR051)	5	H3 + H4 from: Chemistry, Biology, Physics/Chemistry or Ag. Science. (the following combinations are not accepted Biology with Ag. Science or Physics with Phys/Chem).	Not Required
UCD (DN400)	6	O6/H7 in one of Biology, Chemistry, Physics. Phys/Chem, or Ag. Science.	Required.
RCSI (RC001)	5	H4 in Chemistry + H4 in either Biology or Physics.	Required.
RCSI (RC001)	6	O6/H7 in one of Biology, Chemistry, Physics. Phys/Chem or Ag. Science.	Required.
University of Galway (GY501)	5	H4 in two of Biology, Chemistry, Physics, Physics/Chemistry, Agricultural Science	Required.
University of Galway (GY501)	6	O6/H7 in one of Biology, Chemistry, Physics, Physics/Chemistry, Agricultural Science	Required.
UCC (CK701)	5	H4 Chemistry and H4 in either Biology or Physics	Required.

Technically, a student presenting with 480 points in their Leaving Certificate can apply for a place to study Medicine, but realistically points will need to be closer to 580 to have an actual chance of succeeding. Before the points scores are combined, Leaving Certificate Examination points above 550 will be moderated. This moderation was introduced to level the playing field and give students on slightly lower points a greater chance of gaining a place to study Medicine. Leaving Certificate points scored above 550 are divided by 5; for example a student who gains 555 points will have their points moderated back to 551, or for a student with 625 points, their points will be moderated back to 565 points. (*See Table 2 on page 33 for a breakdown of all moderated points).*

The **HPAT** is an admissions test used by the **Irish Medical Schools** for Undergraduate entry into Medicine. All applicants considering Medicine must sit the **HPATs** in the year of expected entry into Medicine. Sixth year students normally sit the **HPATs** in February of their Leaving Certificate year. The **HPATs** consist of three sections.

Section 1: Logical Reasoning and Problem Solving including 44 questions with an allocated answering time of 65 minutes.

Section 2: Interpersonal Understanding including 36 questions, with an allocated answering time of 45 minutes.

Section 3: Non Verbal Reasoning including 30 questions with an allocated answering time of 40 minutes.

It is commonplace for students to attend **HPAT** practice workshops. There are many providers and students need to do research to ascertain which option suits them best.

The max score a student can achieve from the **HPATs** is 300 with **192** a common score achieved. Combined scores for entry into Medicine over the last number of years came in between **729** to **745.**

Student Scenario

*Tom wants to study Medicine and is keen to go to **UCD.** He receives his **HPAT** score in June and obtains a score of 182. Fast forward to August, Tom receives his Leaving Certificate Results and achieves 590 points – Moderated to 558.*

The College offers come in the following week and Tom is relieved as he gets his top choice to study Medicine in UCD. Let's now do the maths on how he received this offer.

*Combined Scores Required to Study Medicine in **UCD** = 736*

HPAT Score	*182*
*Leaving Certificate Points Achieved 590**	*+558*
Combined Total	*740*

**(Leaving Certificate Points achieved 590 moderated to 558)*

In another scenario Tom achieved 182 in the HPATs but his Leaving Certificate Points were lower at 560.

*Combined scores required to study Medicine in **UCD** = 736*

HPAT Score	*182*
*Leaving Certificate Points achieved 560**	*+552*
Combined Total	*734*

**(Leaving Certificate Points achieved 560 moderated to 552)*

Unfortunately in this scenario Tom did not achieve the required score and did not receive an offer to study Medicine in UCD.

In Summary the Process for applying to study Medicine via the **CAO** is detailed here:

- Apply to CAO early November. Receive your CAO number.
- With your CAO Number apply to HPATS early November.
- Normal deadline is mid-January or late application with additional fee early February.
- Engage in Practice.
- Sit Tests in February of Sixth Year.
- Sit Leaving Certificate Exams in June.
- HPAT results available in late June.
- HPAT Scores added to Leaving Certificate Scores and offers via CAO in August.

What to Expect and Qualification

A student entering a Six Year Degree will enter a Pre-Med year with year one spent developing a solid foundation in science related to Medicine. For those entering the five year course they dive straight into their studies in Medicine. All students can expect a broad curriculum from studying biological modules, to chemistry modules and studying medical ethics. Students must be prepared to engage in a lot of self-learning outside of lectures, lab practicals and clinical skills.

Once the student doctor has completed their five or six year course the next stage of the process is to complete a one year internship. This step allows the student doctor or 'Pre-registration House Officer' to immerse themselves in the different specialities of Medicine. The internship includes three months spent in a GP's Practice and the remaining nine months within the different departments of the hospital, including but not limited to, Obstetrics, Paediatrics, Surgery, Psychiatry and Oncology. It is normally during this phase that a speciality is chosen. Depending on the speciality and the level of practice the individual wishes to obtain will determine the next part of the journey. For those considering practicing as a GP they can expect an additional four years supervised training. This training will be completed in both a GP Practice and hospital settings. For those eager to work as a 'Consultant' they can expect to engage in a minimum of three years basic training and an additional six years to reach this specialist level.

Alternative Routes to Qualification

It is no surprise that Undergraduate entry into Medicine is beyond the grasp of many students. For those that are not successful at the **CAO** stage they may consider applying for Medicine via the Post Graduate Route. Once the student has completed their Undergraduate studies, they can then apply for Post Graduate study in the following colleges: **UL, UCD, UCC, RCSI** and **University of Galway.** Entry here is based on competitive scores in the **GAMSAT** Aptitude tests / Personality tests.

Some students opt to study science at Undergraduate level (BSc) to give them the best chance of succeeding at this stage. This is recommended as a sizeable portion of the **GAMSATs** are based around the physical sciences. However, a BSc is not a requirement for Post Graduate entry to Medicine.

Studying Medicine Abroad

To study Medicine in the **UK /NI** you must make a **UCAS** application and complete the necessary assessments which normally involve completing the **University Clinical Aptitude Test (UCAT).** Please note that the UCAS deadline for those applying for Medicine is **October 15th** so it is best to address all necessary steps as early as possible.

Students can apply for four Medical courses via UCAS. Each Medical School in the UK /NI has its own specific entry requirements, but in general, the criteria are: completion of the UCAT, submission of academic grades (Leaving Cert and in some cases Junior Cert), personal statement and a competitive interview. Each college has its unique way of using the results of the UCAT to shortlist those for interview and/or in the final decision making phase. Students need to do their own research on this and can find this information on the specific college websites or via the Search Engine on the UCAS website. (Please refer to the section on UCAS).

Studying Medicine at **Queens University Belfast** is an attractive option for **ROI students.** This is in part due to cross border collaboration, which means that students from **ROI** can avail of the same fees as their counterparts studying in the Republic.

Some students will make the decision to study Medicine in **Europe.** Any student considering this route needs to do in-depth research, reflection and engage with **Eunicas.** Most importantly they need to make sure that the **General Medical Council** and **Irish Medical Council** recognises the course. They also need to bear in mind some of the challenges they could face. While many of the colleges in Europe state that they teach via English, this may not be the case with all lectures. Some students spend considerable time translating notes while trying to keep up with the demands of an exhausting course. Students are advised to gain competency in the language of their chosen country in order to successfully complete their clinical placements. Further to this some colleges in Europe expect students to pay their own professional insurance in order to complete their clinical placements.

Studying Medicine in Italy

While the low tution fees of the Public Colleges in Italy are attractive, getting into Medicine in Italy is hugely challenging. To enter Medicine there, you must sit the **IMAT** Exams. These exams are highly competitive. If you apply for the **IMATS** there is no guarantee that you will even be called to complete the exams. Bearing in mind that only those within the top 10 percent scores will pass and receive an offer, the challenges are clear.

Studying Medicine in Poland and Hungary

With representatives from Medical Colleges in Poland and Hungary visitng Ireland to recruit students year on year, it is no surprise that many students complete their studies in these countries. While minimum subject requirements apply, including presenting with two science subjects, entry is based on external exams in Chemistry, Biology and in certain cases Physics. Applicants may also need to write a letter of motivation and attend an interview. Different deadlines apply to making the application depending on what college you apply to with some students applying upon receipt of their Leaving Certificate results. College fees can be high in Poland and Hungary with some fees hitting the €15,000 mark. However, accommodation and living expenses tend to be low, averaging €400 per month. **(Please refer to section on Eunicas).**

Table 2. Moderated Scoring System Used for Entry into Medicine

Leaving Certificate Points Achieved	Moderated Leaving Certificate Points
551 to 555	551
556 to 560	552
561 to 565	553
566 to 570	554
571 to 575	555
576 to 580	556
581 to 585	557
586 to 590	558
591 to 595	559
596 to 600	560
601 to 605	561
606 to 610	562
611 to 615	563
616 to 620	564
621 to 625	565

Careers in Nursing:

Careers in nursing attract a lot of interest from Leaving Certificate Students, however, uncertainty about what area of nursing to pursue can often cause confusion. The five principal areas of nursing are: **General, Children's (paediatrics), Midwifery, Mental Health (Psychiatric)**, and **Intellectual Disability (ID)**. Nurses work as a key part of the multidisciplinary health care team providing care to patients in all departments within the hospital environment, the community and any institution tasked with the promotion of health, and the prevention of disease and illness.

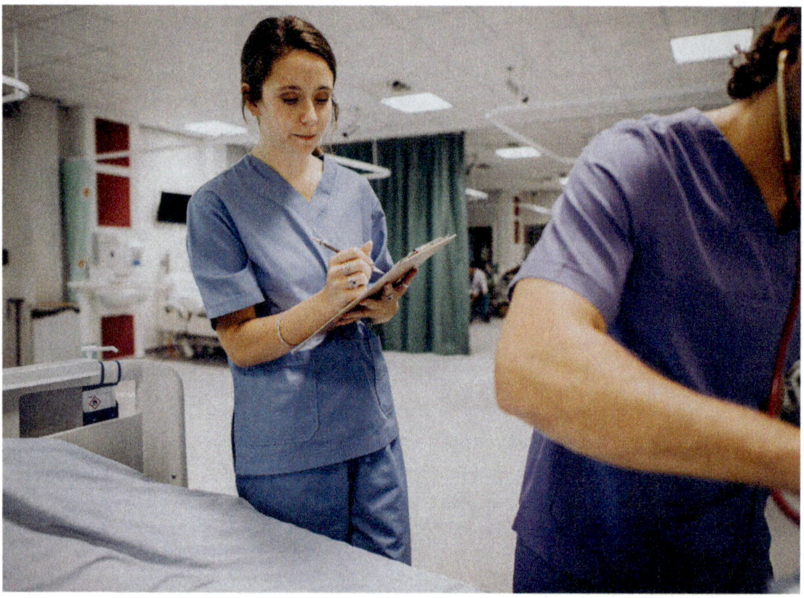

General Nursing:

General Nursing involves working with adults of all ages suffering from long- or short-term physical health conditions. As a General Nurse you may work in any of the departments within the hospital environment including medical, surgical or outpatient's clinics. Nurses also work within the accident and emergency department (A&E) where you may be the first person to assess or "triage" the newly admitted patient.

It is common for general nurses to engage in further studies to advance their careers or to specialise into a certain area, for example, cardiac care, intensive care, oncology care, or theatre nursing.

Advanced training is usually required to provide care in these highly specialised areas, for example advanced nursing practitioner training.

Some nurses work in the community and are referred to as Public Health Nurses while other find their way into Medical Practices where they work alongside GP's and other health professionals. General Nurses working in a GPs practice provide practice care such as wound dressing, blood drawing (Phlebotomy), vaccines and injections. Other duties may Include giving advice, monitoring of pregnant women, or screening of newborn babies.

With experience, nurses may progress into more managerial (Clinical Nurse Manager) or administrative roles within their department or sector. Some may advance into very senior roles such as Director of Nursing for a large hospital. This role is not specific to General Nursing as all nursing roles offer the opportunity to progress into Management roles.

Children's (Pediatric) Nursing: Integrated with General Nursing:

Individuals interested in children's nursing will study children's and general nursing integrated qualification for four and a half years. Nurses in this category will care for newborn babies and children right up to adolescence stage. Children's Nurses work with a wide range of health conditions presented, some of which may be serious and indeed rare. Children's Nurses must also look out for the sick child's family who often need a lot of support and guidance during the child's stay in hospital and thereafter. When children get sick their condition can deteriorate very quickly and they may not be able to communicate how sick they feel. Therefore, the Children's Nurse must have acute observational skills and be able to take action decisively and quickly to ensure positive outcomes.

Neonatology Nurses working in the NICU provide intensive care to premature babies or seriously sick infants. These highly trained specialist nurses normally start their career as a Children's Nurse and engage in further studies to qualify.

Midwifery:

Midwives work closely with doctors and consultants from the Obstetrics and Gynaecology Departments. They are often the lead health care provider to pregnant women. They are responsible for the safe and healthy delivery of a baby and the care of the mother before, during and after labour. Midwives also provide care and guidance for those with fertility complications, those experiencing miscarriage and stillbirth, high risk pregnancy and those seeking termination. Midwives work both in the hospital and in the community with many people now choosing to give birth at home. Due to the nature of the role Midwifery can come with many challenges including managing the emotional, physical, and psychological processes of pregnancy and birth, but for those dedicated to the profession, the rewards of assisting a new life into this world cannot be surpassed.

Mental Health (Psychiatric) Nursing:

Mental Health Nurses care for people of all ages and backgrounds that are experiencing acute mental health problems for example, depression, eating disorders, addictions, schizophrenia, or post-traumatic stress. As a Mental Health Nurse you will support the person in their recovery or help them gain control over their illness. You may help one person to engage in therapeutic interventions, another person to manage their medication and assist another person with social and educational activities.

Mental Health Nurses work in a variety of settings, including Psychiatric Hospitals or the psychiatric unit of a General Hospital. Mental Health Nurses also visit clients in their own homes, supporting and monitoring them through the daily challenges of managing their illness. In recent years Mental Health Nurses have played a key role in the management of illnesses such as Alzheimer 's disease, Dementia, and other related illnesses. Their knowledge and compassion in these areas can often be a source of great reassurance and comfort to families caring for an elderly relative. A trusting relationship and astute monitoring of triggers that may impact the person's life is essential in Mental Health Nursing.

Intellectual Disability (ID) Nursing:

Intellectual Disability Nurses care for people experiencing physical and intellectual disability. The role is as diverse as the cohort you work with, for example you may assist and monitor medications, inspect peg feed tubes for blockage, dress wounds, monitor ongoing physical needs, reduce barriers to independent living, and offer guidance or support through therapeutic interventions. It is a rewarding and interesting role that requires an Intellectual Disability Nurse to work at the speed of their patient and allow this person to develop a new skill and grow in confidence. The majority of Intellectual Disability Nurses work in residential settings within the community. These can include special schools for children affected with intellectual disability, or respite centres and day care centres. The scope of work for an Intellectual Disability Nurse can be quite broad, they can work with people impacted by Down Syndrome, Fragile X Syndrome, Genetic Conditions, and severe forms of Foetal Alcohol Syndrome.

How to Qualify as a Nurse:

Irrespective of what area of nursing is pursued, common Modules within any Undergraduate Nursing Degree will include: Anatomy, Physiology, Pharmacology, Biochemistry, and Microbiology, in addition to Modules in Ethics, Psychology, and Sociology. Clinical placement is integrated into the four years of academic studies. **Table 3** shows the Current Undergraduate Nursing Degrees available to both the Leaving Certificate Student and Mature Student.

Points for entry into Children's Nursing and Midwifery normally are higher than those for entry into General, Mental Health and Intellectual Disability Nursing. Hence, Children's Nursing and Midwifery are often pursued through engaging in Post Graduate studies to qualify. An Undergraduate Degree in General Nursing is often seen as the standard entry requirement to Post Graduate study into Children's Nursing or Midwifery.

Students can also avail of the nursing options offered via the new **Tertiary Degrees** where the student commences their studies with a **one-year PLC** in one of the delegated Education and Training Boards. From there students then progress to complete their nursing qualification over a further four years in a linked Higher Education Provider. Entry to these Tertiary Degree options is based on minimum Leaving Certificate grades but **NOT** Points

Some Students will decide to complete a Pre-Nursing Course via a PLC course with the intention of using their QQI Level 5 grades to apply via the CAO to study nursing. This is a competitive programme with only a very small number of places reserved in the Irish Colleges for those applying via this route. Consequently, students using this route will often apply to study nursing in the **UK** or **Northern Ireland.**

Students can also apply directly to do their Undergraduate nursing training in the UK or Northern Ireland via the **UCAS** system. Entry to these courses is based on the results of their Leaving Certificate. Students considering this route must present with high grades in higher level Biology and English, in addition to minimum grades in higher level or ordinary level Maths. **Please note** some options in the UK require two Science Subjects at Higher Level. The majority of Nursing Degrees in the UK and Northern Ireland are **three years** in duration compared to **four years** in the Irish Colleges.

Alternatively students may consider completing a Level 8 Honours Degree in Ireland, for example, in the areas of Social Care or Public Health Promotion and progress to study a two year accelerated Nursing qualification in the UK. This option is available in all areas of nursing excluding midwifery.

The Hibernia College offers BSc General Nursing with direct application to the college. There are three applications pathways available with Hibernia including **Leaving Certificate Grades, PLC Grades and Mature Entry.** All applicants must complete a series of Aptitude Tests as part of the application process. Fees here are higher than those at the traditional Irish Colleges.

The final option to qualify is to apply via the **CAO** based on mature grounds (over 23 years). Entry here is not based on Leaving Certificate points. Applicants must sit a range of Aptitude Tests and only those with the highest scores will be awarded a place to study. It is a competitive process with limited places reserved in all areas of nursing at the Irish Colleges.

Characteristics of a Nurse:

Nurses are multitaskers, they have to get the job done regardless of what is going on around them and this often involves 'spinning many plates' at the one time. They are at the forefront of care and other professionals including doctors and consultants rely on them to present accurate and detailed information pertaining to symptoms, progress or deterioration of the patients in their care. Indeed, keeping accurate and timely records has become an increasingly important task for the modern nurse.

Nurses must be able to demonstrate confidence and competence in all interactions within the multidisciplinary team. Nurses must be able to communicate effectively at all levels and be able to take specific instructions paying diligence in a fast and sometimes noisy environment. Nurses must have compassion, empathy and excellent listening skills while supporting their patients in what can be a very challenging time. Nurses must be able to observe their patients and be able to analysis their body language to effectively gather concrete information pertaining to the patients' health and to understand their needs. Nurses at all levels deal with stress, trauma and suffering as patients sometimes project their feelings onto the nurse. Therefore emotional awareness is necessary for those considering a career in nursing. Nurses work long shifts; they spend much of their shift on their feet and they have unpredictable eating schedules, so physical endurance and stamina is needed. Nurses must be organised; they must be grounded and have great patience.

The demands of a career in nursing can be challenging, Nurses cover many tasks on a daily basis from caring for their patients, to consulting with peers and superiors. All of this must be done in a calm and efficient manner.

Table 3. Undergraduate Nursing Degrees available via the CAO to both the Leaving Certificate Student and Mature Student

Institution	*Children's Nursing*	*Midwifery*	*General Nursing*	*Mental Health Nursing*	*Intellectual Disability Nursing*
UCC	CK712	CK740	CK710	CK720	CK730
DCU	DC218	-	DC215	DC216	DC217
Trinity	TR911	TR913	TR091 TR093	TR095	TR097
UCD	DN451	DN452	DN450	DN453	-
Dundalk I.T.	-	DK877	DK870	DK874	DK872
ATU Galway	-	-	AU690	AU691	AU832
Galway University	-	GY517	GY515	GY516	-
ATU Letterkenny	-	-	AU380	AU381	-
University of Limerick	-	LM156	LM150	LM152	LM154
ATU, Sligo St. Angela's	-	-	AU991	-	AU992
MTU Tralee	-	-	MT926	MT927	-
SETU Waterford	-	-	SE915	SE914	SE916

Biology Based Healthcare Careers:

The health care careers of Physiotherapy, Occupational Therapy, Speech and Language Therapy, Osteopathy, Chiropractic and Podiatry focus on the study of human anatomy & physiology, the musculoskeletal system and human biomechanics. Hence, biology at Leaving Certificate level is both relevant and important for anyone considering these careers.

Physiotherapy:

The first option in this category is the ever-popular role of a Physiotherapist. A Chartered Physiotherapist is medically trained and will normally be found working in one of our major hospitals. A physiotherapist's role is as diverse as the people they treat. Their key role is to help people regain mobility and function through direct mobilisation, massage, manipulation, electro therapies, and to provide the patient with exercise programmes relevant to their physical condition. They work with patients who are in a stable condition rather than those who are unstable or in immediate danger.

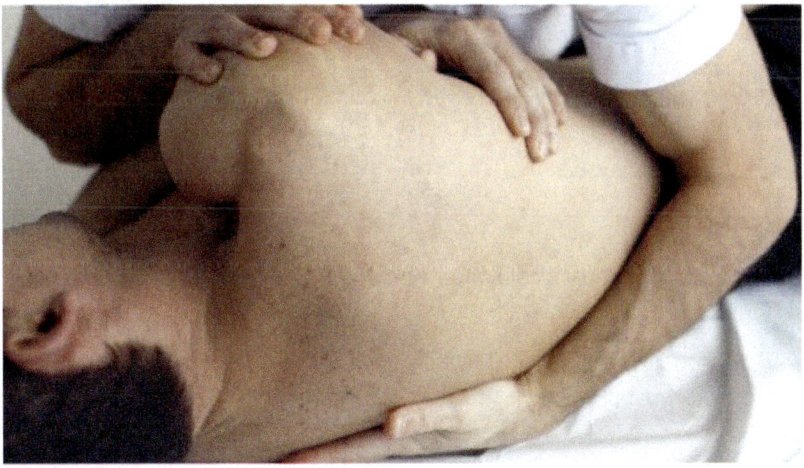

Phyiotherapists manage a wide range of health conditions that impact human movement, mobility and function. Examples of these are brain or nervous system injuries including recovery from a stroke, acquired brain injury, maintenance of conditions such as Parkinson's disease, or lungs and breathing issues relating to cystic fibrosis. They also work with patients experiencing neck, back and shoulder pain, as well as those recovering from sports injuries such as anterior cruciate ligament (ACL) injury. Some physiotherapists may choose to set up and run their own private practice.

There are four Undergraduate Degrees currently available in Ireland to qualify as a Chartered Physiotherapist, with a point's range of 580 to 625 points. The four options are:

Trinity College (TR053) Applicants must present with a minimum of H4 in two of the following: Physics, Chemistry, Biology, Physics/Chemistry, Mathematics or Agricultural Science.
UCD (DN420) Applicants must present with a third language and one lab science subject.
RCSI (RC004) Applicants must present with a third language and one lab science subject.
UL (LM100) Applicants must present with one science subject from: Physics, Chemistry, Physics/Chemistry, Biology, Physical Education or Agricultural Science.

Alternative routes to qualifying in Ireland include the completion of a Level 8 Honours Degree such as Sport Science or Athletic Therapy and Training, and following graduation, the completion of a MSc in Physiotherapy, currently available in Ireland in **UCD, UCC** or **UL.**

Another option related to Chartered Physiotherapy is the career of a **Sports Injury and Rehabilitation Therapist or a Neuromuscular Therapist.** These practitioners treat sports injuries and **are not** fully qualified to work within the hospital environment. Indeed, the majority of these professionals are self-employed people who manage their own practice. Some will be affiliated with sports teams on a contract basis. They specialise in assessing and treating soft tissue problems including muscle pains and strains, as well as treating tendon and ligament strains. They use hands on techniques such as trigger point stimulation, massage, and dry needling to alleviate pain and accelerate healing.

Popular options that lead to qualification include:

DCU (DC204) Athletic Therapy and Training.
SETU Carlow (SE901) Sports Rehabilitation and Athletic Therapy.
TUS Athlone (US956) Athletic and Rehabilitation Therapy.
Portobello College Sports Therapy (Direct Application)

Occupational Therapy:

Occupational Therapists need an in-depth knowledge of the human body, as well as the ability to make meaningful connections with people. As an occupational therapist you will work with people of all ages experiencing various disabilities and injuries including, stroke patients, acquired brain injury, spinal cord injury, physical disability, mental health and educational challenges. You will work in rehabilitation centres, community hospitals, care of the elderly settings and the disability sector. You may also visit clients in their own home. An Occupational Therapist's role is to assist people to recover from major life changing events such as a stroke or a serious motor accident.

Following traumatic events such as those, the Occupational Therapist will play a key role in helping a person to regain independence and dignity. This could include advising and instructing the H.S.E. on adaptations at the client's home, such as improved access to showers or stairs and providing advice regarding other adaptive devices that may be used in the home.

Occupational Therapists also work with young children, for example, assessing the cognitive and motor skills of children with dyspraxia to advise on supports needed to help them engage in education. Occupational Therapists consider all of the person's needs while trying to develop strategies to help them in their current or long term life situation.

There are currently four Undergraduate Degrees available in Ireland to qualify as an Occupational Therapist:

UCC (CK704), University of Galway (GY502), Trinity College (TR054), and UL (LM104).

A third language is needed for both **UCC** and **Galway.**

A minimum of a H4 in one Laboratory Science subject is required for all courses. Recent points ranged from 540 to 600.

University of Limerick is the only option to offer a MSc. in Occupational Therapy in Ireland. It is a competitive route using the **HPATs** and a written English exam as the assessment for entry. Consequently, it is common for students to do their Post Graduate study in the **U.K.**, with lots of options available. Many students going down the Post Graduate route will do an Undergraduate Degree in areas such as nursing, public health promotion, psychology or social care.

Speech and Language Therapy:

A Speech and Language Therapist works with people of all ages from the very young child whose speech is not developing properly, to the older person who may have speech and swallowing impairments due to stroke, cancer or dementia. While many speech and language therapists work in a hospital or community health care setting, others will go into private practice. A lot of the work that Speech and Language Therapists do involves working with young children in the evaluation of speech and language delays and other speech related impediments. They work with children who are non-verbal in the development of alternative communication methods. They are experts in the anatomy and physiology of the throat and voice box. They have an acute knowledge of the psychology of speech and language processing. In school they may have loved English and languages and be referred to as 'very well spoken'. They are patient people and are able to adjust their treatments to work at the speed of their patient. Within your studies you will cover modules in, speech and hearing, social psychology, life stage development, anatomy, physiology, phonetics and syntax. The points are high for Speech and Language Therapy, ranging from 540 to 580 approximately. Here is a breakdown of the courses and relevant entry requirements.

College and Code	Requirements
Trinity College (TR007)	Maths H6/O6. H4 in English or language other than English and O2 in one Science including Agricultural Science, Maths, or Applied Maths. **Or** H4 in one Science including Agricultural Science, Maths or Applied Maths and O2 in English or language other than English.
Galway University (GY503)	Third Language and one Science subject.
UCC (CK705)	H4 in Laboratory Science plus H4 in a third language or Irish.

Post Graduate study is available at **UL** via an MSc in Speech and Language Therapy. The **HPAT's** are used as the assessment tool for entry into this competitive course. Students may engage in Post Graduate study in the **UK** with many offerings available. An Undergraduate Degree in Psychology, Anatomy and Physiology or Linguistics is often recommended as a good baseline Degree for entry into Post Graduate courses in Speech & Language Therapy.

International options to study Physiotherapy, Occupational Therapy and Speech and Language Therapy:

Because points are traditionally very high for these courses in **Ireland,** many students have applied for places on qualifying Degrees in the **United Kingdom.** Although entry is competitive, the entry requirements are usually not as high. Students apply through the **UCAS** system and compete for places in **England, Scotland, Wales** and **Northern Ireland.** Recent changes brought on by Brexit means that it is now very expensive to study in **England, Scotland** and **Wales**, with fees averaging at **£9,250 per annum.** Due to a cross border initiative, fees are not as high in **Northern Ireland**, averaging out at about 50% of their **UK** counterparts. Consequently, applications to **Queens University,** and in particular to the **University of Ulster** have increased over the post Brexit era. Degrees offered by **UCAS** tend to be of three-year duration and come with pre-registration attached.

Entry requirements for **Ulster University** normally require students to have a minimum of H3 in five subjects at higher level including one laboratory science subject. Entry requirements for specific courses can vary so we would encourage all students to check these requirements before applying.

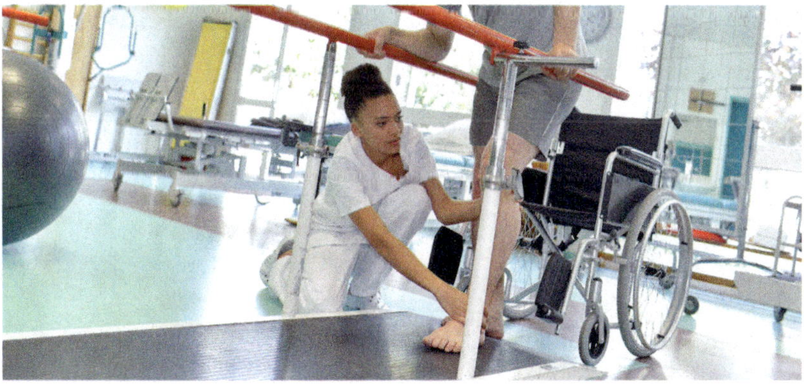

Entry into Physiotherapy is normally the most competitive and many colleges look for two Science subjects. In addition, students are expected to have achieved a combination of H1's and H2's in five or six subjects.

Applying to study Physiotherapy in **Europe** also remains popular with Irish students. This is mainly due to the lower grade requirements and in many cases low college fees. Destinations include **Poland, Hungary, Finland** and the very popular destination of **Groningen** in the **Netherlands.** (Please refer to the section on **Eunicas** for further details).

For Occupational Therapy the requirements for **University of Ulster** are a minimum of H3 in five subjects (non-subject specific). Minimum grades in Maths and English apply. There are many more options to study Occupational Therapy in the **UK.** The requirements are normally H3 in five subjects, including a science subject.

For Speech and Language Therapy there are many available pre-registration Degrees in the **UK.** Requirements tend to be high with some colleges requiring a minimum of five H2 subjects. Students must present with at least one science subject and minimum grades in Maths and English. **Ulster University** require students to present with H3 in five subjects in nonspecific subjects.

While these minimum grade requirements for the **University of Ulster** may seem low, the entry process is very competitive with many students applying for a limited number of positions.

Osteopath and Chiropractic Medicine:

Both these professions treat a variety of musculoskeletal conditions by manipulating and stretching the body and conducting adjustments. The Chiropractor will be more focussed on the spine, conducting high velocity thrusts or adjustments to align the spine and its surrounding muscles, joints and bones. The Osteopath will work with the full musculoskeletal system, conducting stretching and manipulation during their treatments.

Those opting to qualify in these areas will join an established practice to gain necessary clinical experience. These professionals are not normally employed to work within the hospital system, and as such, most practitioners in the Chiropractic and Osteopath areas work for themselves in their own private practice.

Students can study BSc (Hons) Osteopathy at the **Irish College of Osteopathic Medicine (ICOM) in Cork.** The **ICOM** course is not part of the **CAO** system and much of the study is completed on a part time basis. As such this course seems to attract more adults than Leaving Certificate students. It is common for Irish students to go to the **UK** to qualify as an Osteopath. Currently there is no option to qualify in Ireland as a Chiropractor. To study this field, a student must apply through the **UCAS** System to course providers in the **U.K.** (Please see section on UCAS).

For both Chiropractic and Osteopathy options, students will need to present with two science subjects or one science and higher level Maths with grades of H2 and H3 as a minimum.

Chiropodists and Podiatrists:

Chiropodists and Podiatrists care for people's feet. They both deal with issues that might arise with the skin and the toenails, but the Podiatrist can also manage issues surrounding the structure of the foot, for example, plantar fasciitis, bunions or foot deformities. Both will conduct the following: the use of sterile scalpels to treat and remove corns, ingrown toenails, foot calluses and thickened skin. Both offer treatment and advice on the management of conditions like athlete's foot and fungal nails. They can apply liquid nitrogen (Cryotherapy) to freeze and remove verrucae. The majority of Graduates working Chiropody operate their own practice.

The Bachelor of Science (Podiatric Medicine) at **University of Galway, (GY504)** is the only Undergraduate Degree available in Ireland. This is a four-year Degree, which includes the study of the anatomy of the lower limb, podiatric dermatology, lower extremity wounds and microbiology to mention just a few.

Chemistry Based Healthcare Careers:

When qualifying for the careers in **pharmacy, dentistry and dietetics** a good grasp and understanding of Chemistry is required. Indeed most of the colleges providing these Degree courses require that students applying present with **Chemistry at a minimum of H4** or better. Following is a more detailed breakdown of these sought after careers.

Pharmacy:

The majority of Pharmacists work in Community Pharmacies (sometimes called retail or high street pharmacies) and hospitals. However, some may work in the pharmaceutical industry. We are probably all familiar with our local community pharmacist and we often receive valuable information from them about medicines, including how to take them, what reactions may occur and how to counteract these reactions. They also provide services to patients, such as vaccine administration, blood pressure measurement and cholesterol management. With regard to providing vaccination services, pharmacists came to the fore during the Covid pandemic and continue to provide this valuable vaccination service today. Pharmacists must ensure that the medicines prescribed to patients are suitable. Some of these medicines may be stronger than others and may have potential side effects such as in the case of drugs used in the chemotherapy process.

How to Qualify as a Pharmacist:

Pharmacy courses are science focused and applicants must present with Higher Level Chemistry at H4 or better in their Leaving Certificate. Studying Pharmacy can be challenging but rewarding. Course modules include, but are not limited to, Biochemistry, Pharmaceutical Chemistry, Pharmaceutics Formulation Science, Pharmacology, Microbiology, Cellular and Molecular Basis of Drug Action and Toxicity.

Courses are five- years in duration and Graduates are qualified to Master's level **(MPharm)**. Points since the Covid Era have averaged above the 600 mark. Here are the options available:

UCC (CK703). Requirements, H4 Chemistry plus H4 in Physics or Biology plus Third Language
RCSI (RC005). A science subject (H5) from Chemistry, Biology, Physics, Physics/Chemistry or Agricultural Science and a Third Language.
Trinity (TR072). Requirements, H4 Chemistry or Physics/Chemistry plus H4 in one of Physics, Biology, Applied Maths, Geography or Agricultural Science plus Maths at 04/H6.

Note: *Pending accreditation by the Pharmaceutical Society of Ireland, 3 new Master of Pharmacy programmes are due to commence in September 2025. These new 5-year full time courses will provide graduates with the qualifications required to register as practising Pharmacists in Ireland. The new programmes will be launched at Atlantic Technological University, South East Technological University and University of Galway. At time of print course codes were not available*

Pharmacy Technician:

Pharmacy Technicians assist the Pharmacist with dispensing drugs and medications. They process prescriptions, formulate medication, dispense medication, perform pharmacy-related functions, and provide information to customers. They work in community pharmacies and hospital pharmacies. Duties will vary depending on the working environment.

How to Qualify as a Pharmacy Technician:

Courses are two-years full-time study including placement. Points required average from 250 to 350. Chemistry at Leaving Certificate level is **not** a requirement. Completion of the two-year Higher Certificate in Pharmacy Technician Studies qualifies Graduates as fully qualified Pharmacy Technicians. However, there are opportunities to progress on to higher studies such as an Honours Degree in Pharmacy Management and Practice.

Options to qualify as a Pharmacy Technician include: SETU Carlow (SE937),MTU Tralee (MT682), ATU Letterkenny (AU174) TUD Grangegorman (TU654), TUS Athlone (US660).

Completion of a Pharmacy Technician course does not afford Graduates the opportunity to access Pharmacy courses at an advanced level.

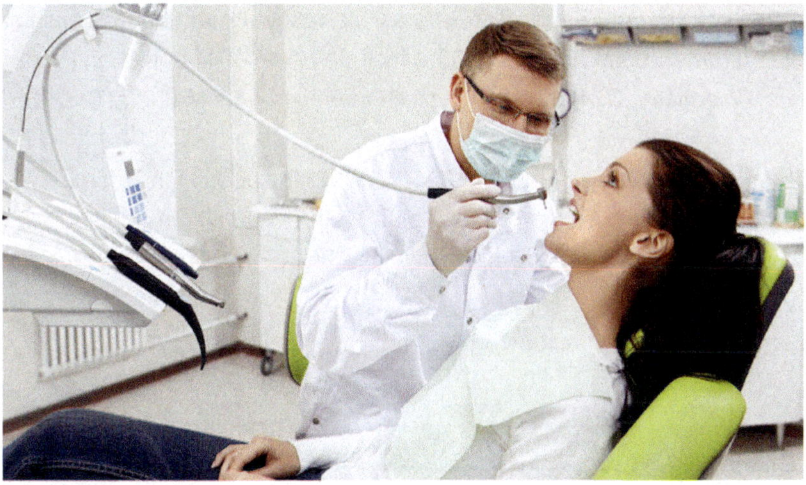

Dentistry:

A Dentist is a physician whose practice is in the field of dentistry. This involves the mouth, teeth, gums and related areas. Check-ups are a major part of the job and they help patients to keep on top of their oral health. In addition to general check-ups, general dentistry involves basic treatments that can be done at a regular dental practice. Such procedures might include filling a tooth, performing a minor surgical procedure such as a tooth extraction, and cleaning and polishing teeth. A Dentist will encourage patients to practice good dental care by brushing and flossing and getting regular cleanings as these good habits can help prevent cavities and other tooth and gum diseases.

How to Qualify as a Dentist:

The B.Dent.Sc. can be studied at **Trinity (TR052)** and **UCC (CK702)** and is five-years in duration. Modules include Dental Pharmacology and Biology, Neuroanatomy and Embryology for Dental Students, Physiology for Dentistry, Dental Pharmacology and a host of other related subjects. Clinical Placement is an important part of this course.

Entry points required for Dentistry are normally around 600. Admission Requirements for **Trinity (TR052)** include H3 and H4 in two of; Physics, Chemistry, Biology and Physics Chemistry plus Maths at 04/H6.

Admission Requirements for **UCC (CK702)** include H4 in Chemistry plus H4 in Physics or Biology plus Maths at 06/H7. In addition, students will also need to present with a 06/H7 in a Third Language (UCC only).

Dental Nursing:

Dental Nurses provide direct support to Dentists with all regular dental procedures. In general, duties will include the decontamination and maintenance of instruments and equipment; as such a key role for the Dental Nurse is to maintain strict hygiene standards in all areas of the surgery. Dental Nurses assist the Dentist with dental procedures, and we are all familiar with the re-assuring presence of the nurse during our visits. In smaller surgeries it's the Dental Nurse that will ensure our records are updated and in some cases making our follow up appointments with us.

How to Qualify as a Dental Nurse:

There are currently options to study on both a full-time and part-time basis. Courses are 2 years in duration with applications to the CAO and, in some cases, directly to the college.

Full time study options available with:

Trinity (TR801).
ATU Letterkenny (AU173).
TUS Athlone (US661).
Applicants will need a Laboratory Science subject. Points can vary from 300 to 400 plus at Trinity College.
Part-time and **full-time** study options at **UCC** with an application directly to **UCC plus an interview** (Level 7 special purpose award).

Human Nutrition and Dietetics:

As career guidance advisors we often encounter a lot of confusion among our clients around the roles of a Dietitian and a Nutritionist. In a nutshell (no pun intended) the main difference between these two similar careers is as follows.

Dietitian:

A Dietitian normally works in a hospital setting and is qualified to give advice relating to food related medical conditions and illnesses such as diabetes, renal disease and heart disease. They may also advise hospital catering staff on dietary requirement of specific patients and how best to meet these requirements. For example, an elderly person requiring surgery may need a boost in calories and protein intake.

How to Qualify as a Dietitian:

To qualify as a Dietitian in Ireland one must either graduate from Ireland's only recognised course at **TUD (TU870)**, Honours Chemistry at H4 required plus high points, or by completing a recognised two-year **MSc** in Dietetics at **UCD, UL** or **UCC** with some students deciding to do their Post Graduate study in **Ulster University.**

Modules involved in studying the BSc in Human Nutrition & Dietetics at **TUD** includes the study of, Clinical Chemistry, Cell Biology, Physiology, Biochemistry, Microbiology, Immunology and Food Studies to mention just a few.

Nutritionist:

Nutritionists are **not** qualified to work in a hospital setting. Hence a high percentage of nutritionists will operate their own nutritional clinics. Others will work in health food stores, while a small percentage will work in the health food related industry, including the development of new food products/supplements, or the research and development of food products such as sports drinks. Nutritionists aim to improve and maintain both the physical and mental health of clients by suggesting appropriate changes to their lifestyle and intake of food, vitamins and minerals. A client could be suffering from conditions such as food intolerance, fatigue, migraine, skin disorders, infertility or chronic sinus infections. Other clients could be training to run a marathon or preparing to play senior inter-county hurling. In this instance the nutritionist will help them gain optimum performance within their sport by advising on diet changes and improvement in consumption and balance of proteins, healthy fats, carbohydrates etc.

How to Qualify as a Nutritionist:

There are a number of Nutrition courses available within the **CAO** system, some of which have high points attached. **It is important to note** that none of these courses qualify Graduates as Dietitians.

Popular courses include BSc's in Nutritional Sciences at **UCD, MTU,** and **TUD.** **<u>We recommend</u>** that you study the content and career progression of all Nutritional Science courses before selection.

Following are some course codes to help you with your research; **(AU172), (AU972), (DK888), (US950), (MT876), (TU872)** and **(DN262)**. Points can vary for these courses from as low as 300 up to the low 500's for some of the Dublin based Degrees.

Sample modules for Nutritional Science courses include the following: Chemistry, Biochemistry, Biology, Food Analysis, Food Nutrition and Health, Plant Based Nutrition, Obesity, Child Wellbeing and Health and Sport Wellbeing and Health.

Technology Based Healthcare Careers:

Radiography, Radiation Therapy, Optometry and **Clinical Measurement** careers have a little more emphasis on technology and often involve the use of sophisticated equipment. However these careers always involve direct contact with patients, and as such can be very rewarding. Learning how the equipment is used and how it functions, is part of all relevant courses. Human Biology will be a part of these Degrees, but a stronger emphasis is on the technology behind the equipment used. Accordingly, we do meet a number of students who like to combine the study of both the body and the latest in medical technological advances.

Diagnostic Radiography:

If you have ever had an X-ray in a Radiology Department it was a Radiographer that was responsible for taking the X-ray. Radiographers work in a Hospital Setting working closely with other Health Care Professionals including Consultants, Doctors and Nurses. The key role of the Radiographer is to produce high quality images of the affected part of the body. Following the scan Radiographers are often called on to assist doctors and other specialists in reading and interpreting the image.

Radiographers work with rapidly evolving technologies and have an interest in keeping up with the latest technology. Radiographers are responsible for producing high quality images including MRI Scans, Ultrasound, CT Scans and Mammograms. Due to the nature of this work, they need to have diligence and acute accuracy in their work.

How to Qualify as a Radiographer:

Currently there is only one Undergraduate Degree in Ireland that qualifies graduates for this profession. The course is offered by **UCD (DN410).** Points tend to be in the low to mid 500's and applicants will need to present with a Laboratory Science Subject plus a Third Language.

Sample Modules include Anatomy/Physiology, Practice of Radiography, Imaging Technology, Magnetic Resonance Imaging, Mechanisms of Disease, and Clinical Practice.

There are a number of colleges offering two-year MSc. top up programmes into Radiography.

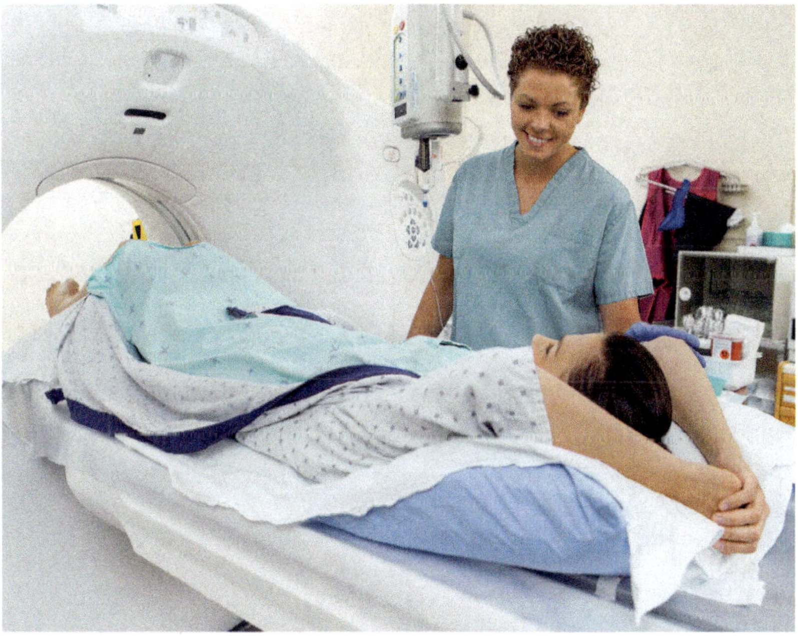

Radiation Therapy:

There is often confusion between the role of a Radiographer and that of a Radiation Therapist. The key role of the Radiation Therapist is in the administering of Radiation Therapy Treatment to patients being treated for cancer. Radiation Therapists work closely with Health Care Professionals such as Oncology Doctors, Nurses, and in some cases, Medical Physicists. They are normally the principal point of contact for patients undergoing treatment for cancer. The chief focus of radiation therapy is in the delivery of high energy radiation to the region of the body where the cancer is present. The purpose of radiation therapy is to destroy the cancer cells without damaging surrounding healthy tissue.

H*ow to Qualify as a Radiation Therapist:*

Currently Trinity College is the only Third Level institution to offer Radiation Therapy (TR055) as an Undergraduate Degree. Applicants will need to present with a Laboratory Science Subject at higher level – H4. Points range tends to be in the low to mid 500's.

Sample Modules include Anatomy, Physics for Radiation, Biochemistry, Physiology, Cancer Care, Communication and Psychology, and Clinical Practice.

UCC is the only college in Ireland that currently offers a top up MSc in Radiation Therapy

Optometry:

Many of us have been to the Optician for an eye test. The Optometrist in this practice is the Primary Eye Care Provider. Optometrists are Healthcare Practitioners who work independently or collaboratively in a health care team. Optometrists work in High Street practices, hospitals, and primary health care centres. There are opportunities to specialise in specific areas for example, in low vision management.

How to Qualify as an Optomestrist:

To qualify in Ireland as an Optometrist one must have completed a four-year BSc. Honours Degree in Optometry at TUD Dublin (TU871) or alternatively study abroad.

Applicants to this course in TUD must present with a Laboratory Science Subject and at least an O3 in Mathematics. Due to the subject matter being studied within this Degree **we normally recommend that applicants should be good at Maths, and we also recommend Physics as being the ideal Science Subject** to have as a foundation for the course. Indeed having two Science Subjects would be an advantage.

Currently there are no Post-Graduate courses in Ireland leading to qualification as an Optometrist.

Clinical Measurement:

Clinical Measurement Physiologists work in one of five disciplines – Neurology, Respiratory, Vascular, Gastrointestinal or Cardiology. They are a vital part of the inter-professional team looking after patients. For example, eleven of the top twenty acute medical presentations require the skills of at least one of the clinical measurement disciplines.

Clinical Measurement Physiologists are Healthcare Practitioners working directly with patients, performing, reporting and acting on diagnostic tests and investigations. As such the emphasis of their work is in the preparation and administering of medical tests.

Clinical Measurement Physiologists are responsible for monitoring and upkeep of most of the measuring equipment used in modern hospitals. They also have a key role in the upkeep of critical equipment such as ventilators and respirators. Most of this work is hospital based but there are increasing opportunities to work in the community with the development of community based diagnostic hubs.

How to Qualify as a Clinical Measurement Physiologist:

There are currently two Honours Degrees that qualify Graduates to work as Clinical Measurement Physiologists:

TUD BSc. Honours **(TU868)** and **ATU Sligo** BSc. Honours Degree **(AU973)**. Points for these sought after Degrees are normally between 450 and 500.

ATU Sligo also offer a Post Graduate qualification option via their Master of Science in Clinical Measurement Physiology. For entry, a Science Degree with a high content in Mathematics is required.

Chapter Four

Psychology and Social Sciences

Careers in this sector encompass the following: Social Work, Social Care, Youth Work, Psychology and Counselling/Psychotherapy.

Social Work:

A Social Worker is a professional who works with people who are suffering forms of abuse, neglect, and discrimination. Much of the work they do is with families in crisis, particularly in child protection. Their role is to ascertain the needs of this person through interviews, observations and evidence-based practice. Once these needs are established, the Social Worker will work alongside other relevant professionals to develop a care plan for the individual. They are also charged with monitoring the implementation and progress of the care plan. A Social Worker will not work with the client on a daily basis but rather meet them at regular intervals to establish progress and monitor ongoing further needs. This career involves administration and competency in writing reports, in addition to being able to build a trusting relationship with the client. This trusting relationship is the corner stone to the care plan being developed and implemented.

Top Tip: For anyone (regardless of age) considering a career in Social Work it is recommended to gain meaningful experience working with vulnerable people. Social Work can be very rewarding but often quite demanding.

How to Qualify as a Social Worker

The Bachelor in Social Studies in Social Work **(TR084)** at **Trinity College** is the only Undergraduate option that gives the full qualification and accreditation to students who wish to go directly into Social Work. Points for this course are approximately 470 year on year. Within this course you will study core Modules in Psychology, Sociology, and Social Policy and Legislation. This course allows Graduates to apply for registration with **CORU**, the Health and Social Care Professionals Council, an essential part of practicing in Social Work.

For those wishing to qualify in Social Work via a Masters in Social Work, they normally start by studying a three or four year Bachelor of Social Science (B.Scs.) Degree. There are currently strong options in Irish Universities including **UCC (CK102), Maynooth (MH107)** and **SETU Waterford (SE920).** Another popular option is UCD's Social Policy and Sociology Degree, (DN750).

Aspiring Social Work Master's Degree hopefuls must ensure that **Social Policy** is a core component of their Undergraduate Degree. Where an Undergraduate Degree is lacking in Social Policy Modules, there are a number of Social Policy conversion courses that can be completed in order to achieve the requirements to apply for the Masters of Social Work.

Mature Student Entry into Social Work:

For those over the age of 23 years they can apply via the CAO to UCC for the Bachelor of Social Work (BSW) which is specifically tailored towards adult learners.

Other Social Science Degree options:

Social Science Degree is broad by nature and can lead to a variety of career paths other than Social Work. The emphasis of a Social Science Degree is very much focused on People Sciences for example Sociology which attempts to analyse social trends across modern societies. Hence it is often quite a useful Degree for those aspiring to work in our public services in the areas of administration and our large Civil Service organisation in Ireland.

Graduates often top up their Social Science Degree with a Master's in Social Research and then target high level research positions with organisations such as the Economic Social Research Institute **(E.S.R.I.)**. Hardly a week goes by in Ireland without the publication of new research from this highly regarded institute.

The Bachelor of Social Science Degree at **UCD, (DN700)** has a vast array of subject combinations available, and students can take two subjects in a Joint Major Honours Degree which opens many doors to potential future careers.

Social Care:

There is often confusion about the role of a Social Worker compared to a Social Care Worker. Qualified Social Care professionals work with vulnerable people on a daily basis. They work in a very practical manner to help these people to overcome the challenges that they face. Much of the work that Social Care Workers do in Ireland involves working with people with intellectual disability, young people in care, the elderly and the homeless. Depending on the sector you work in will determine your daily duties, but these could range from practical physical assistance to helping with organising social and educational activities. This may involve rota work, including weekends and evenings, however, this would be dependent on the sector you work in.

While Social Care Workers report that their profession gives them great satisfaction and makes a dramatic difference in people's lives, it can also be a challenging and physically demanding career.

How to Qualify as as Social Care Worker:

To qualify as a Social Care Worker is relatively straight forward with most of the Technological Universities offering a B.A. Applied Social Studies or a B.A. Social Care Practice. Points required for these courses are approximately 300.

Popular Degree courses include:
TUD, Grangegorman Campus **(TU996).**
TUS, Limerick Campus **(US920),** Athlone Campus **(US921).**
SETU, Carlow Campus **(SE918),** Waterford Campus **(SE919).**
ATU, Sligo Campus (AU918).
Dundalk Institute of Technology (DK862).

There are options to gain employment in this sector with a Level 7 Ordinary Degree. However, the Level 8 Honours Degree opens up better options and opportunities to progress to team lead, care and case management, and management of services.

Youth Work:

Youth work addresses the overall wellbeing of the young person including educational, psychological, emotional and physical needs. Youth Workers strive to ensure young people achieve their potential in a supportive environment. They work with young people in the age group from eleven to twenty-five. In this role you could find yourself advocating for young people in the community or facilitating interventions for young people to enable them to discover and develop their identity. Youth Workers allow young people to have a voice and to be active members in their community.

How to Qualify as a Youth Worker:

There are a range of study options available to CAO Applicants.

NUIM Community and Youth Work as a full time **(MH116)** or a part time **(MH803)** study options. Due to the nature of Youth Work, an interview is normally part of the application process.
TUD: (Blanchardstown) Community Development and Youth Work L8 Honours Degree **(TU992)** and Level 7 Ordinary Degree **(TU792)** Options.
Dundalk IT: BA in Community Youth Work L7 Ordinary Degree **(DK767)** Interview plus one year add on to L8 - Applied Youth Work **(DK866).**
UCC: BSocSc (Hons) (Youth and Community Work) – (CK114) available to Mature Students over the age of 23 years.

Psychology:

As humans, we are always seeking to understand ourselves and others; hence Psychology can be a popular choice for students. Psychology is the scientific study of human behaviour. We often say that when a student takes a Degree in Psychology, they learn about themselves in addition to learning about how people think, perceive and act.

For those who wish to pursue a career as a Psychologist, they must be prepared for long term academic studies and training. This journey is by no means straight forward, and only those with determination should engage.

How to Qualify as a Psychologist:

There are many options to study Psychology, but the main criterion to meet is that the course taken is fully accredited by the Psychological Society of Ireland (PSI). This is necessary when it comes to pursuing Post Graduate study and training to qualify as a Psychologist. The majority of courses in Irish Universities and Technological Universities have this accreditation but always check. For those who decide to study psychology via the BA Arts Degree route (combining Psychology alongside another subject) they must complete a PSI accredited Psychology Conversion course should they wish to pursue Post Graduate Psychology training.

Points for Psychology Degrees always come in on the high side and nearly always requires 500pts plus at any of the seven major Irish Universities. SETU Waterford and Dún Laoghaire Institute of Art, Design and Technology (IADT) have popular options with full PSI accreditation also. These courses normally require entry level points of approximately 400 to 450.

Post Graduate Studies:

When we think of a Psychologist working with a patient we normally are thinking of a **Clinical Psychologist.** The role of a Clinical Psychologist is to assist people who may be experiencing mental health issues on either a short or long term basis. This can include the diagnosis of mental health illnesses such as for example, Depression or Schizophrenia, and recommending treatment and or medication to help alleviate the symptoms.

Educational Psychology is another area that we get asked lots of questions about. Educational Psychologists typically work for the Dept. of Education and are best known for carrying out Educational Psychology assessments on young people. Where conditions such as Dyslexia and Dyspraxia are suspected, the Educational Psychologist uses a series of scientific tests to calculate the severity of the condition. Many second level students engage with Educational Psychologists by completing Educational Psychology assessments either through the school system or privately.

Qualifying as either a Clinical or Educational Psychologist can take a very long time. Both of these professions require the completion of a three-year PhD Doctorate prior to attaining full recognition. Consequently we advise students to be prepared for a course of studies that can be anywhere from nine to eleven-years. Indeed, qualification as an Educational Psychologist also requires candidates to have a minimum of two years' experience working as a Primary Teacher.

Occupational or Work & Organisational Psychology is another popular area and one of the shorter routes when it comes to qualifying. Working primarily in the Human Resources and Consultancy fields, Occupational Psychology normally needs a time commitment of around six years before full qualification is attained.

Finally there are other areas, for example **Sports Psychology** and **Forensic Psychology**, with Post Graduate options available in **Ireland** and the **UK.**

Please note a Degree in Psychology does not make a Psychologist. It can be quite difficult to find employment with just a Psychology Degree. Some will find employment working in the Social Care areas (see Social Care Careers) while others may transition into more administrative type roles within the public service. Others will engage in alternative Post Graduate studies, with Primary Teaching, Speech and Language Therapy, and Business/ Human Resources being popular choices.

Counselling / Psychotherapy:

Being a Counsellor is a career more suited to adults. Some of the courses leading to qualification have a minimum age limit of twenty-six years prior to entry. Many Counsellors and Psychotherapists remain in alternative employment while they grow and develop the client base for their practice. The significant difference between the Counsellor and Psychotherapist is how they practice. Psychotherapists work with deep-seated problems including mental illnesses and personality disorders. Counsellor's work tends to address adjustment difficulties, situational or personal problems. Psychotherapist training is normally offered at Post Graduate level, while a Level 8 Honours Degree can lead to qualification as a Counsellor. The regulations governing practicing as a Counsellor/ Psychotherapist have changed over the last few years and more changes are expected. However, the **minimum** academic requirement now is a Level 8 Honours Degree for both professions. Once the initial training has been completed, a period of supervised practice must occur before the Therapist is considered fully **accredited.**

Those considering a career in this area need to be aware that it is not a quick transition. It takes many years of academic study and training as well as a challenging accreditation process. Once qualified and accredited, most Counsellors and Psychotherapists become self- employed and enter private practice

The Caregiver Archetype :

The work in these caring advisory (caregiver) roles as described above will involve engagement and immersion into people's lives, their vulnerabilities and in many cases the most intimate part of their existence. A special type of person is suited to these careers, including those with the ability to make a deep human connection, to listen not only to what is being said, but to observe a person's body language, expressions, and behaviours, to assist and support the person through their crisis. The ability to make informed observations without being judgemental is very important in these roles. This gives the professional the ability to help and support the client in situations where their circumstance cannot be changed but can possibly be improved. The ability to know your professional boundaries especially around confidentiality is hugely significant.

Leaving Certificate students would sometimes comment that they often find themselves caring for their friends when on a night out, **talking** their friends down from a crisis, or **intervening** with friends who have had a falling out. These attributes and abilities accurately describe the archetypal behaviours associated with caring and advisory careers. However, one must always bear in mind the strict codes of conduct that need to be taken and observed when dealing with vulnerable people. While we won't cover these in any great detail here, suffice to say that Degree studies in these areas will emphasise the importance of adhering to best practice principles.

Chapter Five

Law

Along with Medicine, careers in Law have been seen as among the more prestigious careers that students pursue. They are viewed as an attractive option and appeal to those with an eye to a career with lots of responsibility and strong financial rewards. Students studying Law in Ireland will normally qualify with a Bachelor of Civil Law **(BCL)**, or a Bachelor of Legal Letters **(LLB)**, while others study Law through a Bachelor of Arts route **(BA)**.

What can be expected when studying a Law Degree? Well primarily intense work, exhaustive reading, in-depth research, and developing your skills in mooting. Modules including: Constitutional Law, Family Law, Employment Law, Property Law, Criminal Law, Law of Tort, Intellectual Property Law, and Legal Ethics will form the core of any Law Degree. Students will also study Criminal Codes, Law Journals, and Law Books. They analyse previously presented Law cases and learn how to proficiently summarise and present this information.

On completion of a Law Degree Graduates normally continue their studies in order to qualify as either a Solicitor or Barrister in Ireland. Qualification in both professions can require a good deal of motivation as the journey to qualification can be sometimes competitive, somewhat long and indeed expensive.

Solicitor:

The trainee Solicitor will commence their journey by completing entrance exams to the **Law Society of Ireland,** referred to as **FE1 Exams;** they must also at this stage secure a two year apprenticeship within an approved Solicitors practice. In addition to engaging in this apprenticeship, they will also study Professional Practice Courses **(PPC1 and PPC2)** before completing and hopefully passing the related Exams **(FE2 and FE3)**. The good news for the trainee Solicitor is they are paid during the apprenticeship phase with some Solicitor practices offering to fund their courses and exams. This qualification process normally takes approximately three years. Many newly qualified Solicitors will remain within the practice where they completed their apprenticeship and start their full professional career as a salaried trainee Solicitor. Some Solicitors may go on to specialise in a specific area of Law, for example Criminal Law or Family Law, while others will remain in general practice.

Barrister:

Law Graduates (with approved Law Degrees) who would like to become Barristers continue their journey by taking entrance exams to **Kings Inns.** To be accepted on to the professional **Degree of Barrister at Law,** Graduates must have passed certain core Law Modules in their Law Degree. Please refer to Kings Inn for a list of **recognised courses.** The next step is studying for the **Degree of Barrister–at–Law** with **Kings Inn** over a period of eighteen months. This is followed by a period of **pupillage** for one year, where they work under the instruction of a Lead Barrister or Master. This pupillage period is unpaid but it gives the trainee Barrister the opportunity to fine tune their skill set, build professional networks and gain professional exposure. Once qualified, Barristers become self-employed and are tasked with promoting their skills and reputation within the legal world in order to establish their practice and move from Junior Barrister to Senior Counsel Barrister. This career move normally takes over ten-years to achieve. The majority of Barristers will operate from offices within the **Law Library** at the **Four Courts** in Dublin.

Studying Law

There are a plethora of options to study Law including, pure Law Degrees, Law and Business, Law and Languages, Law and History, Law and Politics, or Law and Criminology. We will now introduce some of these options:

Trinity College provide an **LLB (TR004)** or **BA** route with options in Law, Law and Business, **(TR580)** Law with German **(TR019)**, or French **(TR018)**, Law and Political Sciences **(TR582)** or Law and History **(TR581)**. Points are normally high at the **Trinity Law School** and can range anywhere from 550 up to 625.

University College Dublin (UCD) have a broad range of Degrees in Law. Options include Business with Law **(DN610)** or the **BCL (DN600)** with options in Irish, Economics, History, Politics, Philosophy, Social Justice, and French. **UCD** also offer their unique **BCL/Maîtrise** via **(DN600)** dual Degree with students spending two years in Ireland and two years studying Law at a **French University**. This course is taught via the medium of French. Law is always a popular option in **UCD** so students will need high points to be successful in gaining a place. Points ranging from 560 to 625.

Dublin City University (DCU) offer a **BA in Economics, Politics and Law (DC230)**. An interesting course and popular choice for students as it is broken down into equal proportions of study in each area. However, this mix of subjects may not provide enough Law Modules for students wishing to pursue training as a Solicitor, and most definitely a Barrister. **DCU** also have options to combine Law as a Joint Honours **(JH)** Degree **(DC292)** with History, Languages or Media Studies via their Humanities Department. **A Bachelor of Civil Law and Society (DC232)** is also available. Points vary depending on the route you chose with the **JH** option lowest at around 400, while up to 500 will be needed for the **BCL**.

Maynooth have the option to study for a **BCL (MH502)** with Accounting, Business, Languages or the very popular choice of Criminology. They also offer a **Bachelor of Legal Letters (LLB) (MH501)** . Points at Maynooth tend to be lower than their city counterparts with points generally between 430 to 475.

University of Galway has a very strong Law faculty and their **BCL in Human Rights Law (GY252)** is a very popular choice. Galway also have options combining Law with Business **(GY250)**, or their pure **BCL (GY251)**. Points again are on the high side ranging 500 to 540 plus.

Maynooth University (MH101), University of Galway (GY101) and SETU Waterford (SE200) also offer applicants the opportunity to study Law via their **Bachelor of Arts Degree**. This route allows students to combine Law with a wide selection of other subjects. These **BA Degrees** offer a vast range of subjects to choose from as well as great flexibility to build your Degree of choice. Arts Degrees have lower points thresholds and over the past number of years students needed points in the region of 300 to 350 to qualify for a place. Arts at Maynooth **(MH101)**, Galway **(GY101)** or SETU Waterford **(SE200)**, can be a good option for students who have a general interest in Law, but who have not decided on whether they will be pursuing careers as Solicitors or Barristers.

University of Limerick (UL). A popular option with students is an **LLB in Law (Law Plus) (LM029)**. This is due to the broad range of electives that you can study alongside Law, plus the engagement in Lawyer skills and the opportunity in year three to avail of an eight month work placement. **UL** also has an **LLB in Common and Civil Law (LM027)** and the option to study a **BA in Law and Accounting (LM020)**.

University College Cork (UCC) provide students with great options to study Law. Options include studying a **BCL (CK301)** over three years, or to continue for an extra year with a pathway into **Clinical Law**. The Clinical Law programme provides either a work placement in the legal provision, or the pathway into **International Law** providing the opportunity to study abroad for one academic year or semester. **UCC** also has options to study a **BCL** alongside: Business **(CK307)**, French **(CK302)** and Irish **(CK304)**. Due to students being attracted to study Law in UCC points again prove to be high, specifically Law and Business at 550+ with other options ranging 500 to 550.

Technological University Dublin (TUD) offerings in Law include a **BSc Business and Law (TU904)** with points averaging around 450. **TUD** also offers an **LLB Degree (TU917)** with French, German or Spanish as well as offering a full **LLB (TU918).** Law at TUD will normally come in between 400 and 450, but the Law options with Languages can be significantly lower at between 350 and 400.

There are a range of lower point Law Courses available that should be up for consideration on a student's **CAO.** A student could study an LLB at **SETU** Waterford **(SE404)** and Carlow **(SE405)** with a point's range of 300 to 320. In addition **SETU Carlow** have an excellent option to combine Business and Law **(SE403)**. **Technological University of the Shannon (TUS)** in Athlone allows students to combine Law with Business **(US848)** and in Limerick to combine Law with Taxation **(US849)** with points ranging from 300 to 350.

Both **Griffith College (GC403)** and **Dublin Business School (DBS) (DB568)** have a long and proud tradition in the education of aspiring legal professionals. Many practicing Solicitors and Barristers started their career with fully recognised Degrees conferred at either of these colleges. Because **DBS and Griffith College** are **private fee paying colleges** they do not attract students at the same rate as their public college counterparts. Consequently entry point levels are significantly lower at around 250 points for their Level 8 Honours Degrees.

Students interested in studying Law but not in pursuing careers as Solicitors or Barristers need to be aware that it can be challenging for Law only Graduates to gain employment. However, there are opportunities for Law Graduates in the area of Legal Executives. Legal Executives carry out a broad range of activities in supporting Solicitors and Barristers in the preparation of legal documentation. Persons interested in this role can gain recognition by completing further studies in this area.

Probably the most popular option for Law only Graduates is to work in the business sector. As such we often recommend Law and Business as a viable option for students who have an interest in Law but also like the world of Business and are attracted to the many different career areas it presents.

The Legal Archetype:

The debaters, the negotiators, the persuaders, the communicators, the people who love the written and spoken word are aligned with careers in the legal profession. The ability to articulate, to research, to be methodical in establishing the facts in any given situation, are all skill sets necessary in this area. People attracted to this world would cringe when they believe someone is making assumptions based on hearsay. They need to research and have factual information in order to arrive at a decisive conclusion or make a judgement. They want to work with people and make differences in people's lives but they want to be rewarded and recognised for this. It is often said that people in these legal professions like the finer things in life, good wine, fine dining, five-star hotels, first class travel, so therefore they want to be financially rewarded for their work in order to manage this lifestyle. However, Legal Professionals must have great integrity and adhere to legal ethics, as this is the corner stone to their practice and reputation.

Shy retiring types should stay clear of these professions. The Legal Professionals have to put themselves out there; they have to be confident to stand in front of their peers, superiors, and in some way put on a performance. In addition to this they must be social beings, as socialising with your peers is necessary particularly when you are starting off in your career in order to build a strong professional network around you and establish your place in a competitive legal world.

Chapter Six

Business

Business Studies:

When a client chooses Business Studies as their first choice, we are always happy for them (and their parents). The reason for this is that we know they will end up with strong employment prospects. We often remark that the only reason a Business Graduate isn't working in a business-related position is because they don't want to work there.

This good news story continues when it comes to researching your Business Courses at college. Every University and College in Ireland have solid offerings when it comes to studying Business. Most Degrees are structured similarly and include the following broad outline.

Business Degree - Structure & Options:

Years One and Two Core Modules.

For first and second years, students are given a broad introduction to Core Business topics including Accounting, Economics, Human Resources, Marketing, Management, Business Maths, IT, and Enterprise.

Most colleges also offer **Business International** routes. If studying Business International courses students select a language to study alongside their Business Subjects. A lot of courses require the student to have studied the language to Leaving Certificate standard at Higher Level. We feel that it is important that students taking the language option should be comfortable with the language they are choosing, as it can be a large part of the subjects they study. Typical Language Options include French, German, Spanish, and sometimes Chinese or Japanese.

When students select Business with a Language or International Business, they normally spend their Third Year studying abroad at a partner University. For students who take Business without the language there are normally valuable Work Experience opportunities available during Year Three.

Business Degree - Final Year:

Students get to select their preferred major option, and these majors are generally chosen from the following topics:

- **Accounting**
- **Management**
- **Marketing**
- **Economics & Finance**
- **Human Resources**

* Some colleges may differ from the above list. It is important to research what major options are available before choosing your Business Degree. Choice of major area will largely determine where each Graduate will seek employment.

Careers in Business

Careers in this sector are varied and numerous. For the purposes of this chapter, we break Business Careers into two main categories:

A. Careers in the Business & Financial Services Sector

B. Careers in the Business Management Sector

Let's take a look at the Financial Services Sector first. Examples of careers in this sector include:

- **Financial Services including Banking and Insurance**
- **Economist and Stockbroker**
- **Accountant and Accounting Technician.**
- **Financial Analyst**
- **Fund Accountant**
- **Budget and Credit Controller**
- **Invoice and Debtors Clerk**

The Financial Services sector is consistently strong, and many Graduates get their first taste of careers in Business in this sector. There are good salaries to be made and extra effort made on the job is generally rewarded with bonus payments and promotion opportunities. Management opportunities also exist for ambitious Graduates with experience.

To qualify for jobs in the Finance areas many students start with either a solid Business Degree as described above or sometimes students choose a more specific Degree such as Accounting and Finance, if they already know the direction they wish to pursue.

General Business Degrees:

There are many Business courses to choose from in Ireland, so many in fact that it would be very difficult to list them all here. In the following section we will list some of the more popular Degrees available to students.

The majority of Business Degrees are referred to as **BBS (Bachelor of Business Studies).** Exceptions include the **Bachelor of Commerce (B.Comm)** Degrees at **UCD, UCC & NUIG**. The B.Comm Degrees are essentially the same as their BBS counterparts.

Business Degrees which include the study of a Third Language are mostly referred to as Business International or B.Comm International Degrees. **Please note** that some colleges offer a Business International pathway that does not include the study of a Third language.

One of **Trinity College's** main Business offerings is the four-year B.E.S.S. Degree **(TR081)**. This course has a strong emphasis on Economics and includes study options in Law, Politics and Social Studies. Global Business at Trinity **(TR080)** is the other major Business Degree on offer from that College.

Global Business at DCU is an exciting Degree that involves the study of both Business and a Language. The course is unique in that it offers two-years of study at **DCU**, and two-years abroad in the country where the language is spoken. This course also provides **work experience placements in both countries.** Language choices on offer include French, German and Spanish. **DCU** also offers to students the possibility to use the same structure to study in the U.S. and Canada (no Third language studied). These courses are very popular and consequently entry points tend to be high averaging around the mid 500's and upwards in some cases.

Business Degrees at **DCU (DC111)** and **University of Limerick (LM050)**, are noted for their highly sought after work experience placements on their regular Business Degrees, called **INTRA** at the respective colleges. **UL** is the only Business course that offers a specialism in Risk Management and Insurance Studies.

The B.Comm at **UCD (DN650)** is one of Ireland's best known Business Degrees and has lots of major options to choose from. Because it's a Dublin University, points can be high, normally in the 500 plus category. The B.Comm's at **UCC (CK201)** and **NUIG (GY201)** are also excellent; however **UCC'S** major options are a bit different to their counterparts and should be researched thoroughly prior to selection.

TUD Business and Management **(TU903)** is a slightly lower point option for those seeking to study in Dublin, while **Maynooth University** also offers a solid Business Degree with options **(MH404).**

All of the Technological Universities have a range of courses at Levels 6, 7 and 8. The Level 8 Degrees are normally in the 300 points region. **SETU** Waterford is very popular with students applying for Business Degrees in the Southeast **(SE400).**

Specific Accounting and Finance Degrees:

For those who already know that they wish to fast track their career into the world of Finance, then there are some great options available within the **CAO.** Probably the most popular of these are pure Accounting or Accounting and Finance Degrees. These courses offer Graduates generous ***exemptions*** from required add-on studies to qualify as an Accountant. Some notable course options include Accounting and Finance at **DCU (DC115), TUD (TU922)** or **Maynooth University (MH407).** Students can also apply for Accounting at **UCC (CK202)** or **SETU** Carlow **(SE407)** or Waterford **(SE408).**

Some students like Economics and are attracted to the world of Global Markets and Stocks and Shares. It is possible to study Economics through a variety of routes. Some of the better-known options include Economics at **UCD**, take Economics as a single Honours Degree **(DN710)** or study it with another subject through Social Sciences **(DN700).** TUD **(TU905)** has a solid Economics Degree with options to complete your Degree over three or four years. **UCC** offers Economics **(CK212)** and Maynooth has two options **(MH415 and MH416)**.

Economics and Finance at **UCD (DN670)** is highly sought after as a Degree, and applicants will need to be around the 600 points mark to be successful. We categorise this course as part of a family of Degrees within the ***Financial Maths*** area. Applicants will need to present with at least a H4 in Maths for entry and these courses are a combination of Financial Modules and pure Maths. Financial Maths Degrees can be a good foundation Degree for progression into high paying positions such as Financial Analysts and Actuaries. Both **UCD (DN203)** and **DCU (DC126)** have direct entry routes into Degrees in Actuarial Studies. Good Financial Maths course options can also be found in **DCU (DC127)**, **UL (LM058), UCC (CK407)**, and **University of Galway (GY309)**.

Please note DCU's (DC127) gives students the opportunity to explore Actuarial Studies and Financial Maths prior to specialising into their chosen option in Year Three. (Specialising into Actuarial Studies via this route is grade dependent)

Business Management Careers:

There are a number of careers which require a good fundamental grounding in Business disciplines, and careers in this sector often involve more contact with people. Careers on the **People side of**

Business involve a lot of organisational skills, and appeal to those who like structure and keeping on top of things. Sometimes these careers bring a variety to the job as managing new projects can be an important part of the brief, especially for those that venture into management positions.

We like to call this sector the **People side of Business** or **Business Management**, and specific jobs in this sector include.

- **Marketing, Sales, & Event Management**
- **Customer Services and Call Centre Operator**
- **Administration / Secretarial**
- **Hotel and Retail Management**
- **Human Resources Management**
- **Business/Enterprise Management and Entrepreneurship.**
- **Property Management/Real Estate**
- **Careers in the Public Service (Civil Service)**

Business Management Courses:

These courses are a combination of Core Business Subjects combined with a range of Specialist Modules that support the specific career area, for example, Human Resources or Marketing. The Subjects Human Resources and Marketing are among the main topics studied in Leaving Cert Business. Within Business Management courses, core subjects such as Accounting & Economics in a lot of cases are not covered in as much detail as in general Business Degrees.

Here is a brief overview of what is entailed within each of the sectors:

Marketing:

Marketing is often seen as the more creative side of Business, and there is definitely scope for ***ideas people*** here. Marketing is often closely aligned with Sales and there is an ongoing strong demand for Sales Executives. However, Marketing is more about developing a demand for a product rather than just selling it. Market Research or **defining your niche** are key components in any marketing role and this can involve.

- **Analysing the competition**
- **Defining your target market**
- **Learning about this audience**
- **Determine your unique selling point (USP)**
- **Create a Marketing Strategy Plan**

The Marketing strategy/plan used will be determined upon the market research and the target audience but may include:

Using creative skills to brand the company or if you like personifying the Business such as designing (or collaborating with a Graphic Designer) to design logos, and slogans. You may find yourself liaising with the Accountancy department to implement a pricing strategy that is comparable to competitors. While some Companies Marketing plans are best served by using traditional Marketing techniques such as advertising on TV, Radio and Newspapers, more common techniques include Digital Marketing such as running social media campaigns, managing, and updating creative content on websites, or even app development. A Marketing Professional may find themselves tasked with managing public relations, for example writing press releases and tracking and monitoring media coverage of a new product or an event. A big part of Marketing is managing Google Ads and Analytics; this allows the Marketing Professional to evaluate that the Marketing strategy/plan is working and reaching the target audience, or what needs to be changed in the plan.

The Marketing role does not end once a product is sold, or an event is finished; at this point it is all about maintaining customer relations and increasing customer retention and brand loyalty through high standards of follow-up and customer service.

TUD provides an excellent range of Business Management Degrees, including their very well-established Degree in Marketing **(TU922)**, while **SETU** Waterford has an exceptionally good Marketing and Digital Media Degree (SE410) at very attractive points.

Human Resources (HR):

Strong people skills are the hallmark of successful professionals in the Human Resources area as these managers spend a lot of time working with people. Demand for HR Professionals has increased in recent years, particularly in large organisations, as the challenges of managing a large workforce become increasingly complex. Smaller companies such as **SME's** don't tend to hire HR Professionals on a full-time basis, preferring to utilise the services of an experienced HR Consultant on a as needed basis.

To qualify as a HR Professional, you can study a Business Degree and major in HR, or for those who are certain they wish to pursue HR they can avail of pure HR Management Degrees at **TUD (TU906)** or the **National College of Ireland, (NCI)** Dublin **(NC005).**

Public Service Administration - Civil Service:

A sizeable percentage of the workforce are employed by the Government of Ireland within what is referred to as the Civil Service. The emphasis of a Civil Service role is one of Administration and appeals to those who like to keep on top of things and who like a structured working environment. Key skills for the Administrator include having strong organisational skills and a sense of control over their work. They also love the sense of security that goes with most if not all roles within the sector.

Roles are as varied as the Departments that they serve. These can be as diverse as **Foreign Affairs** in another country to the person one would meet in the **Department of Social Protection**. The **HSE** has a huge administration function, while Local Government offices such as in County Councils are also part of these public service structures.

Just as the roles and Departments are very varied so are the entry routes. One can access the Civil Service at Clerical Officer Level which has a minimum entry level of Leaving Certificate, while the holder of a Level 8 Honours Degree may enter at a higher Administrative Officer level.

There are no specific Degree requirements for entry into the Civil Service. However, in some cases, should a Graduate seek entry into a technical role such as IT or Accountancy, then a qualification relevant to the area being applied for would be necessary.

Hotel Management:

If you have a love for travel, customer service and working with people, then Hotel or Hospitality Management might be for you. Add in a smattering of languages and a liking for organising events and then you are definitely on the right track. Variety is definitely a feature of this at times in a demanding role with no two days being the same.

However, **just a word of caution**, hotels tend to be busiest around weekends and holiday periods, hence you will need to adjust your lifestyle to working ***out of hours***.

The Shannon College of Hotel Management is Ireland's best known Hospitality Management training college. Situated near Shannon, it is a purpose-built training college that offers two Honours Degree programmes **(GY261, GY262)** in this field. Entry on to these courses requires applicants to have a Third Language, as well as attending an interview at Shannon with points awarded based on performance at interview. The effort is worth it however as Shannon College boasts ***Full Employment*** for all its Graduates since, **believe it or not, 1951!**

Other colleges that provide Level 8 Degrees in this area include **ATU** Letterkenny **(AU322)**, and **ATU** Galway **(AU630)** as well as **SETU** Waterford **(SE921)** and **TUD (TU952)**. The Technological Universities also offer a range of Level 7 Degrees that lead to qualifications in this sector including **Dundalk IT (DK750)**.

Other options allow students to combine Hotel Management with either Tourism Studies or Event Management.

Property Management and Estate Agent:

The world of the Real Estate Professional can be varied and rewarding. Variety in this career comes from being out and about, viewing, evaluating, showing and finally selling a wide range of properties. Good people skills are really important as working in this demanding career will require you to build strong relationships with a wide variety of clients and Companies. For a person who likes buildings, and houses in particular, the world of real estate has a lot to offer.

When we think of Real Estate, we normally think of large organisations such as Sherry Fitzgerald or your local Auctioneer on the High Street. While most Graduates set out to find employment in these areas, a small number also find employment in the management of large Office/Apartment complexes in our larger towns and cities. Some specialise in the Agricultural sectors such as Marts, or indeed the selling of agricultural land. However, all of the sectors require Graduates qualified in Property Management/Real Estate.

Property Management including Real Estate Studies can be studied at both **TUD** Level 8 **(TU836)** and Level 7 **(TU731),** and **TUS** Limerick **(US882).**

Retail Management:

If you are interested in the world of fast paced consumer goods, then Retail Management could be a good choice for you. If you enjoy the challenge of being busy and are good at organising, then these skills are in demand in major Retail outlets.

While many of the nation's large Department Stores have ***in-house*** training routes that lead to promotion, **TUD** does offer the countries' only Level 8 Honours Degree **(TU925). SETU** Waterford also offers a Level 7 Degree in Fashion Buying and Retail Management. **(SE419).**

Useful Subjects for Business Degrees:

Work is generally numeric, and you will need to be comfortable with numbers and indeed computers for roles with more of an emphasis on Finance. Key subjects in all Business courses include Accounting, Economics and Business, and a good ability or interest in these subjects is a definite advantage. However, it is important to point out that entry on to a Business Degree **does not** require a candidate to present with any Leaving Certificate Business Subject.

Business careers are very reliant on Information Technology, and so you will need to be comfortable with the use of Computers, and in particular, Spreadsheets such as Excel.

Note: Using computers in this context does not involve any type of programming or software development.

The Business Archetype:

The Business, Finance and Administration sectors are made for the Business Administrator Archetype. They show a true appreciation of what numbers mean and are extremely well organised around them. They love their post-it notes and highlighter pens and can't imagine work without alphabetically indexed and colour coded lever arch files. They populate the Banking, Insurance and Fund Accounting Corporations of this country.

For this type, there is nothing more attractive than tidying up and reorganising a set of messy accounts, whipping them into shape, and transforming them into a set of clear tables and categories. Many take the long and often challenging route to becoming a qualified Accountant, while others will venture into Management positions where they are often quite successful. Here, they can now fully utilise and expand their organisational skills into organising other people.

A Minister of Finance embodies the key traits of this archetype. They might be often background players to a leader, but what they lack in charisma they make up for in capability. Their number crunching and their level efficiency are what organisations and state finances rely on to keep running.

Working in the Public Service also appeals to these Business Administrators. Not only due to the emphasis which is placed on structure, and a clear demarcation between Departments, but also very importantly the security and predictability that working in a Government Department or Local Authority brings.

The People Planner and Enterpriser:

The world of Business is also populated by the Planner and Organiser Archetype. People motivated by this type of work love an event. We could call this category of employment **buzziness**, as there nearly always seems to be a buzz associated with the related work activities they do. We find them organising conferences and weddings in major hotels or managing fast paced retail outlets and leisure centres. They love interacting with people and are ideally suited to roles in customer services and direct sales.

In Finance, we often find them as qualified Financial Advisors, giving one-to-one advice regarding mortgages or life assurance. Image is fundamental to this bracket. They like to wear classic cuts and keep it sharp, a contrast to their strong but considered approach to people. They look the part and they act it. They are generally positive and enthusiastic about life and work, and one tends to feel uplifted in their company.

As students however the planner organisers don't always show a high level of motivation for study. While academically bright, the routine of school and study doesn't hold much appeal for this **on-the-go personality.** They are often hard to tie down and sometimes we must be prepared to move with them to spend time in their company. People from this archetypal range often bring their optimistic outlook to Enterprise, where they are naturally good at Marketing and Sales. Many have a leaning towards starting their own business and become self-employed. When they do so, they can often become quite successful.

Chapter Seven

Gardaí, Defence Forces, Emergency Services and Pilot.

Each year a strong cohort of students show interest in these careers. For those considering these areas we advise lots of research, including speaking to those already working in these sectors, and if possible by gaining some work shadowing/experience. Most importantly interested parties need to be aware that they will have to go through a rigorous and competitive recruitment process in order to be successful with their application.

__Garda Síochána:__

The recruitment drive for An Garda Síochána is advertised via the **Public Jobs** platform. All interested parties should set up their **Public Jobs Account** and register their interest on this platform. As part of the selection process applicants will engage in various stages including.

Stage 1: The Completion of an Application Form.

Stage 2: Applicants will be invited to complete a set of aptitude tests including numerical and verbal assessments. There are a range of tests presented at different levels.

For example, a Numerical Test question could involve the candidate being presented with a sequence of numbers **1 , 5 , 9 , ? , 17,** and then asked to answer what is the missing number in the sequence.

Stage 3: Only those who are successful at the aptitude test stage will be invited to attend an interview. This interview will assess your ability in different competencies including, but not limited to:

- **Conscientiousness**
- **Resilience**
- **Interpersonal Skills and Service Ehos**
- **Exercising Authority**
- **Using Information and Problem Solving**

There is also a Simulation Exercise used as part of the interview process.

Stage 4: If successful at the interview you will be called for a medical and physical fitness test. The current **Eyesight requirements** are a minimum distance vision of 6/18 on eyes that can be corrected to 6/9 and 6/12 or better with glasses or contact lenses if necessary.

Successful candidates will commence their two-year training programme in the **Garda Training College in Templemore**. This training is broken down into three phases, with the final phase allowing the probation Guard to work independently. With some years' experience and in most cases some specialist training, the Garda can apply for a place in one of the many different units within An Garda Síochána. Examples of specialist units include Detectives, Criminal Assets Bureau, Traffic Corps and Forensics. There are many promotion paths available to Gardaí also, from Sergeant up as far as Commissioner.

Until 2022 those joining An Garda Síochána had to be proficient in two languages, one of which had to be Irish or English. This is **no longer** a requirement and proficiency in only one language is required.

Army, Navy and Air Corps:

There are two levels that individuals can join the Army, Navy or Air Corps.

Cadetship: Those considering this route must present with a minimum of a H5 in three Leaving Certificate Subjects and they must also present with a Third Language. Similar to An Garda Síochána it is a competitive and challenging recruitment drive with an excess of applicants compared to positions available.

Army Cadets will engage in officer training, studying and working their way towards becoming a commissioned officer and taking command and responsibility for their branch/unit. In the Army this could entail the leading and commanding of a platoon of soldiers on Peace Keeping Missions.

Naval Cadets normally follow one of two distinct career paths. One path is referred to as the operations Pathway and the emphasis here is towards navigation and command of a naval vessel. **Pathway number two** is more of a technical role with a lot of emphasis on Engineer ing, for example, Mechanical or Electronic Engineering. Indeed it is popular for qualified Engineers to join the defence forces at Graduate level.

The main roles of the Irish Navy are in Fisheries Protection, Search & Rescue and keeping our shorelines free from smuggling of illegal drugs.

Air Corps: For those lucky enough to join the Air Corps at Cadet Level they will train to become a pilot. Air Corps pilots are trained to fly a variety of military aircraft including Helicopters. Entry into the Air Corps can be very competitive and a good ability in Maths is a prerequisite for scoring high on the admission tests. There will also be a number of specific interviews to be passed for those that come through the aptitude tests.

Recruits will join the General Services within the Army, Navy and Air Corps, and upon successful completion of basic training will be awarded the position of Private Two, progressing to Private Three with further training, and progressing to specialist training thereafter. In the Army or Navy you may have the opportunity to complete Apprenticeships, or upskill into areas such as Electronics or IT. You may also get the opportunity to qualify in Personal Training. In the Air Corps you may get the opportunity to complete qualifications In Alr Craft Maintenance. To qualify to train as an Aircraft Mechanic you must meet the entry requirements for General Engineering (Level 7) at **TUD.**

All vacant positions are advertised via www.military.ie. The recruitment process is similar to An Garda Síochána, including: Completion of Application Form, Successful Completion of Aptitude Tests, and Interview & Medical.

Paramedic Training:

Student Paramedic Training is available through the **HSE,** with the **HSE** also managing the recruitment process. All positions are available on the **HSE** website or via the **Public Jobs** platform. Interested parties should set up their **Public Jobs Account** and register their interest in this training programme. The recruitment process is similar to that outlined previously under An Garda Síochána, including, Application Form, Aptitude Testing, Interviews, and Medical and Fitness tests. Applicants must present with a Science Subject at Leaving Certificate Level or a recognised **QQI** Award in Science. You must also be the holder of a full unendorsed **Class C1 Driving Licence** upon application (this allows you to drive a minibus for up to 16 people). (Please refer to the **HSE** website for more detail on the exact requirements).

If successful in the recruitment drive you will commence your Paramedic training over four academic years. Successful completion of all assessments and examinations in year-one is required in order to progress to the remainder of the programme.

Alternatively students could consider **University of Limerick's** four year Bachelor of Science in Paramedic Studies **(LM103)** or UCC's four year Bachelor of Science in Paramedicine (CK708). A full unendorsed Class **C1 Driving Licence** is required for both courses. Applications are made via the **CAO** as normal.

Fire Services:

Vacancies for all positions within the fire services are handled and advertised by the Local Authorities, for example, Wexford County Council or Dublin City Council. The main criteria for those considering these roles are they must live and work within a reasonable communicating distance to their designated Fire Stations with some Stations stating a one mile radius to their designated Fire Station. Some members of the Fire Services will be employed in other fields of work and therefore are members of the Retained Firefighters, being on call to respond to emergency calls.

Retained Firefighters are fully trained and paid for their work. They are normally required to be available for a minimum of twenty-four weeks per year, and to respond to the emergency pager regardless of what task they are involved in at that time. Some members of the Fire Services are employed on a full time basis; this would be particularly evident in the larger cities.

In general terms applicants will complete an Online Application Form, be called for Interview, complete some form of Psychometric testing and if successful, be placed on a panel. Members of the panel will then complete a medical and physical fitness test and successful candidates will fill arising vacancies within their Local Authority area. Due to the nature of the job, candidates must be physically fit and strong and possess emotional strength. Once recruited you will begin training, including; Firefighter Induction Training, Breathing Apparatus Training, Emergency First Responder Training, and Fire and Rescue Training.

Interested parties should present with a minimum of a pass in five Leaving Certificate Subjects including Mathematics and English. **Prior** to the commencement of training candidates must hold a current full and unendorsed **Category B Driving License**, as they will be required to drive emergency vehicles

Commercial Pilot Training:

Every year we get a small number of students who show an interest in qualifying as a Pilot. Some of these students have researched the various pathways to becoming a pilot and many have taken some flight lessons in light aircraft

The options to qualify as a pilot include completing an Apprenticeship with one of the Airlines for example, Ryanair or Aer Lingus. As both these options are highly competitive with minimum positions available, it is often the case that interested parties will have to go the private training route. There are a number of private training schools with **Atlantic Flight Training** in Cork remaining poplar. The private training route is expensive, with fees approximately **€100,000.**

For those considering Pilot training but are perhaps a little unsure they could consider a College Degree with the option of Pilot Training integrated. For example, **DCU (DC117)** offer Aviation Management with pathways to Pilot Studies or Air Traffic Controller Studies. **MTU (MT946)** in Cork offer an ab-initio programme that provides embedded Pilot Training as part their Degree in Global Business with Pilot Studies. It is important for students to be aware that as part of the Pilot Training aspect in both above mentioned courses there will be additional fees extra to the normal college fees that apply. Applications for both these courses are through the **CAO.**

SETU Carlow in collaboration with **FTEJerez** offer a Bachelor of Science in Pilot Studies **(SE715)**. A competitive selection process is in place for this option. Applicants will apply directly to **FTEJerez**.

Chapter Eight

Sport

Careers in Sports are attractive to students heavily involved in playing sports, from those who play hurling and football to those who participate in cycling and swimming, and also those *Gym Buddies* who love lifting heavy weights. These students want to perfect their skill in their chosen discipline, and they are also interested in helping and teaching others to improve their competitive edge. They are often influenced by what they observe in their own training sessions, or what they see by watching top sports people achieve in their sport.

There are of course advantages and disadvantages of working in Sports and students need to work out what is most important for them. Yes, technically you may get the chance to work with top sports people, however this is a very niche area, and the reality is that for many students it is probably unlikely to happen. Working in Sports is a competitive area that provides fresh challenges every day. It is a results business and you are only as good as your last competitive outing. You work at what you love, you are active in your job, and you are not completely tied to a desk. However, for the majority who enter a career in Sports, their hobby is no longer their hobby, and due to the nature of the work, their work commitments can often clash with participation in their own Sport. This is often a big **NO** for students.

We break Careers in Sport into four broad areas: Sports Recreation and Leisure Management, Sports Science (Coaching and Training), PE Teaching, and Sports Injury Treatment and Rehab.

Detailed breakdowns of PE Teaching and Sports Injury Treatment are covered in detail in the Sections on Teaching and Biology Based Therapies respectively. In this section we will cover the other two remaining areas.

Sports Recreation and Leisure Management:

The majority of work in this sector is in privately or publicly managed gyms or leisure centres. Some may work in outdoor activity centres. There are jobs available in this area but wages and opportunities for promotion tend to be average. Where you work, and the level you work at will determine your responsibilities, but in general terms you will advise clients on how to use the equipment in the gym, demonstrate proper procedures when lifting weights or perhaps facilitate fitness classes such as aerobics. You may work on a one-to-one capacity with a client via personal training, offering guidance and support on effective workouts and nutrition. Administration tasks are part of this role, including managing the reception area of the gym, ensuring gym memberships are up to date and paid. In a managerial role you may be responsible for hiring staff, managing staff rosters, developing marketing campaigns, and sourcing new and up to date equipment for the gym. For some who study this area they may find employment with sporting bodies such as the **GAA** working purely in administration.

Many of the courses in Sports Recreation and Leisure Management are available in the Technological Universities with low points attached. Here is a flavour of what is available:

MTU Cork Campus level 7 option **(MT510).**

TUD Grangegorman Campus level 8 **(TU955).**

TUD Blanchardstown Sports Management and Coaching **(TU935).**

SETU Waterford has a level 7 **(SE933)** and a level 8 **(SE906)** option.

TUS Athlone Campus **(US952).**

ATU Mayo Campus has an option to study Outdoor Education and Leisure at level 7 (AU692) and level 8 **(AU590).**

There are also options available at some of our major Universities including **UCD (DN430)** points coming in at the high 400s, and **UL (LM105)** with points in the low 400s.

Regardless of where you study Sports Recreation and Leisure Management, it will be a mix of Business-related Modules such as Marketing, Human Resource Management, Financial Management, plus Science related Modules including the Physiology of Sport and Exercise,

Anatomy of Sport, and Sport Psychology to mention just a few. Having Biology plus a Business-related Subject at Leaving Certificate Level is advantageous, while exam P.E. is also useful.

Sports Science Careers:

Studying Sports Science in college is mostly Science based and covers areas such as Physiology and Anatomy, Sports Psychology, The Biomechanics of the Body, Nutrition, Strength and Conditioning, Sports Injury, Player Development, and Coaching Techniques and Fitness and Movement. While students tend to enjoy these courses, the opportunity to enter employment in the area of coaching and training is very restrictive. Sports Science Graduates are primarily qualified to improve performance through coaching and training teams and individuals. Because of this most coaches work on a contract basis.

Graduates are largely looking at becoming self-employed, meaning that the individual will have to be prepared to start their own business. The nature of this work means that you will work unsociable hours and your working life will often clash with your sporting and training regime should you be involved in playing competitive sport yourself. This is a prospect that many sporty students are not keen on. The majority of students that we see who are keen on studying Sports Science are generally into playing sport at a competitive level. They are often attracted to the major colleges by the prospect of being selected for their teams to play in prestigious competitions such as the **Fitzgibbon** or **Sigerson Cups.**

Of course, you do not have to play sports in order to study Sports Science. Indeed, some of sports greatest and most successful coaches were not great sports players themselves.

There are a number of Sport Science courses available including options at:

University of Limerick (LM089).
Dublin City University (DC202).
University College Dublin (DN425)
Maynooth's Sport Science with Health **(MH221).**

Points are high for these options with **DCU** and **UCD** in the mid-500s and **UL** and **NUIM** high 400s. Students must present a Laboratory Science Subject to meet entry requirements. **NUIM** also offers a Business with Sport Science Degree **(MH412)**, points have been in the high 400's, however a Science Subject is **not** required.

SETU Carlow gives students the option to study their long-established **Sports Coaching and Business Management** course. This option allows students to focus on their chosen sport, choosing from Gaelic Games, Rugby, or Football with both level 7 and level 8 courses available. Entry into these options is based on Leaving Certificate points, the presentation of a portfolio and the completion of an interview and skills test. SETU Carlow also provides a Sport and Exercise Science Degree (SE905) at mid-400 points, and Strength and Conditioning (SE903) in the high 300 points range.

There are a number of other lower point courses available at the Technological Universities, including:

ATU include options at their Galway Campus **(AU662)** and **(AU664)**, Letterkenny Campus **(AU320)** and **(AU222)**, Sligo Campus combining Sports with Business via **(AU903)** at level 8 and level 7 **(AU804)**.

ATU include options at their Galway Campus **(AU662)** and **(AU664)**, Letterkenny Campus **(AU320)** and **(AU222)**, Sligo Campus combining Sports with Business via **(AU903)** at level 8 and level 7 **(AU804)**.

MTU Kerry Campus **(MT913)** and a higher point option **(MT915)** at the Cork Campus.

SETU Waterford Common Entry BSc in Sport and Exercise Science **(SE902)**, affording students the option to branch into Nutrition and Exercise, Sport and Exercise or Health and Exercise. They also have Sports Coaching and Performance **(SE904)**.

TUD Tallaght have both level 8 **(TU936)** and level 7 options **(TU736)**.

TUS have options at level 8 and 7 including: Athlone Campus **(US957)**, **(US951)**, at level 8 and (US788) at level 7. Limerick Campus **(US945)** level 8 and **(US640)** at level 7. Thurles Campus **(US958)**, **(US959)** plus other level 7 options.

So as you can see, there are many options available for students that want to commit to studying how high performance sports techniques are continually raising the bar, and pushing competitive sports on to higher and higher levels. Whether there will be as many openings for people on graduation is an entirely different matter. While there is a continuous strong demand for coaches in all sports and at all levels Ireland, unfortunately it is the reality that the vast majority of these are volunteers and as such are not making a living from their passion.

Chapter Nine

Media, Journalism, Television, Film and Acting

Journalism:

In our practice we sometimes meet people that have an amazing ability to move others with the power of their words and their command of the English language. Good journalists can have an immense influence on our daily lives through their writing prowess. Whether through reading their daily newspaper columns, listening to engaging radio shows or to our favourite podcasts on social media, Journalists help us to keep informed regarding our interpretation and understanding of the world. Journalists help us paint pictures of events that affect our daily lives. These events can range from Political upheavals to issues around Law and Order, and from International Wars to memorable Sporting Occasions. Journalists are often referred to as **News Reporters** and they populate our national and local newspapers. More recently with the growth of Television and Radio, **Broadcast Journalists** have come to the fore. As a sector, Journalism has experienced major changes in recent years as we gravitate more and more to the world of online news. However, despite the changes, Journalists still do what they love most, which is using the power of the written and spoken word to formulate opinions and influence others.

Apart from caring DNA, Irish people are known for their writing abilities. There are too many world famous Authors to list, but the tradition continues with modern day contributors who will one day contribute to the canon of literature.

How to become a Journalist:

DCU has a long tradition in training Journalists and they offer two Degree options. One option is their BA in Journalism **(DC132)** which provides a strong grounding in writing for news. The second option is called Communications **(DC131)** and this course has a little more emphasis on what is termed ***Broadcast Journalism***. Both of these three-year Level 8 Honours Degrees average around the 400 – 450 points mark. Staying in Dublin **TUD (TU985)** offer a BA in Journalism at lower points.

Outside of the capital **University of Limerick (UL)** offers it's popular BA in Journalism and Digital Communication **(LM039)** while the **University of Galway** offers Journalism through Irish in its strong Cumarsáid Degree **(GY122)**. Points for these courses tend to be more in the 350 – 400 range.

Finally **Dublin Business School (DB565)** has a BA in Journalism at approximately 250 points. **This course is not part of the free fees initiative.**

Creative Writing:

A cohort of students who have a gift of writing, an imaginative and creative mind-set and ability with the English language may lean towards the area of Creative Writing. Careers in this area are diverse, with some Graduates entering the world of Publishing, Authoring and Editing books, Script Writing and Editing, Advertising, Content Creation, Copywriting, or even Public Relations. Getting established in an associated career can have its challenges and determination and grit are needed to succeed in this imaginative and innovative world.

Some Graduates enter this world through a combination of Subjects via Arts Degrees, including English, Literature, Classics or Drama Studies. However, in recent years it has become more common for students to study specific Creative Writing Courses.

There are fewer jobs than qualified applicants in pursuit of these jobs, but persistence pays off for the Creative Writer if they appreciate the process along with the outcome. Linguistic intelligence is inclined to play a more dominant role within the world of the Writer, but it is nonetheless an important part of the family of Creative Careers.

There are a small number of Degree options available including:

The **University of Galway's** BA in English and Creative Writing **(GY111)** allows students to focus on these two Subjects plus the study of another Arts Subject of their choice. One of the main attractions of this course is that students can be mentored in their writing by established Irish Writers in Year Three.

UCD's BA in English and Creative Writing **(DN530)**. Students can also choose from a range of different Modules including, but not limited to, Drama Studies, Film Studies and Languages. Established Irish Writers work with students on this course and provide invaluable insights into the writing process.

ATU Sligo's BA Writing and Literature **(AU929)** also has a good focus on Creative Writing and remains a popular choice with students. Professional mentoring and workshops facilitated by established Writers is a big draw for this course.

Film and Television Studies

Film and Television is an area that has attracted a lot of interest from students in recent years. With a significant increase of blockbuster movies in our cinemas and the constant stream of TV mini-series' across an ever-growing range of streaming platforms, it is not surprising to see the piqued interest. However, the gap between watching a good movie to that of writing, producing or directing one is substantial, and is often a bridge too far for many. Nevertheless this does not seem to deter students from applying to study Degrees in this fascinating field in Ireland today.

For those lucky enough to gain employment in the world of Film and Television, the roles are as varied as the genre of film or series being made. Some may enter Technical roles including operating studio equipment such as Cameras, Sound and Lighting, or Studio Mixing and Editing. Others may enter roles in Writing, Directing and Research. Many of the courses reflect these varied roles, and Modules will focus on these Subjects. Students will also get a thorough grounding in the history of film, helping them understand how film has helped shape the world we live in today.

> Similar to a lot of the Creative Areas finding a job as a Filmmaker can be challenging. Many Graduates of Film/Television courses find that opportunities in Ireland are quite limited.

The following is a list of course options available to applicants:

Trinity (Joint Honours): Study Film alongside one other subject. (Traditionally high points).

TUD (TU983): Film & Broadcasting. Specialisms available in Production and Directing. Very strong content with points around the mid to high 400's.

Maynooth University (MH109): Media Studies. Study Film/Television alongside an Arts Subject

University of Galway (GY127): Film & Digital Media.

IADT/National Film Centre (DL843): Portfolio and Interview required as part of the selection process.

There are a range of other Level 8 Honours Degrees available including:

Dundalk IT (DK770), **ATU** Galway (AU615), & Letterkenny (AU230, Level 7), **SETU** Carlow **(SE734)** and TUS Limerick **(US807)**. Points for these courses tend to be in the 300 bracket.

Ballyfermot College of Further Education. QQI Level 5 (Portfolio and Interview required), **Non-CAO.** Direct Application to **BCFE**.

UCD (DN520) and **UCC (CK105)** also offer a BA in Film Studies. These courses focus mainly on giving students a good understanding and appreciation of Film

Drama and Theatre Studies:

As Careers Advisors we set out to give impartial and balanced advice relating to all career areas. Giving a balanced view means that we highlight both the advantages and disadvantages associated with the career choice being considered.

For careers in the world of Theatre and Drama the major disadvantage is finding a secure job that pays enough to sustain a person in the modern world. It is a well-known fact that for even those people who find a position as a Professional Actor, many struggle to earn a decent living.

Because of this many Actors confine their pursuits on the stage or set to part time or indeed voluntary roles while supplementing their income with alternative paid employment. However, the pull of the Theatre and satisfaction of playing a leading role is extremely strong among these creative individuals and they are prepared to give this career every chance, despite the obvious pitfalls.

For those who wish to pursue full time studies in this area, there are a number of course options available to them.

UCC (CK112): Drama and Theatre Studies (International Pathway).

UCD Arts & Humanities (DN520 and DN530) Drama Joint Major with Film and Music Options.

Trinity (TR025): Drama and Theatre Studies with options available.

Trinity also offers places on its Acting course through the well regarded **LIR Academy.** Entry to this option is hugely competitive. Students apply directly to the Academy with a demanding audition used to whittle down successful candidates. There are a range of courses and levels available including, Degree, Foundation and Post Graduate study.

University of Galway (GY118): Drama, Theatre and Performance.

Mary Immaculate College, Limerick **(MI010)**: Applied Theatre Studies.

Griffith College Dublin. Leinster School of Drama provides a range of courses geared towards those who would like to Teach Drama on a Professional level.

Gaiety School of Acting. This renowned college provides a full range of Full and Part-Time Acting courses with direct entry to the School.

Additional Stage Design, Acting, Theatre Courses to consider:

ATU Sligo Performing Arts Acting **(AU931 and AU824)**: with Theatre Design stream linked to the **Abbey Theatre.**

SETU Carlow Set Design & Construction available at Level 8 **(SE734)** and Level 7 **(SE735).**

Chapter Ten

Music

We are forever amazed at the amount and depth of the musical talent that is evident in Ireland. Almost every student that presents to us, lists music as an interest, whether as an instrument player, singer or even just as a listener. Many are involved in local music groups and, through competition, have experience in performing from a local Feis right up to the National Concert Hall. However, for a variety of reasons very few go on to committing to careers as full time Musicians or Singers. Lots of musically talented students seem to decide at an early stage that playing music for money is far too competitive or risky for them. They prefer to keep it as a hobby or use their talent to perform with local Musical Theatres and Societies. They love the buzz of opening night and the work they put into their performance is often on par with that of Professional Artists.

When we discuss careers in Music we break it down into three general categories, which are, Music Teaching, Music Technology and Sound Engineering, and Music Performance.

A detailed breakdown of Music Teaching is covered under the Chapter entitled Careers in Post Primary Teaching. In this section we will cover the remaining two areas.

Music Technology and Sound Engineering:

If you have an interest in creating, recording, mixing and editing music then you might consider studying Music Technology and Sound Engineering. It is common for students who are considering this area to have some background in mixing music or perhaps to be doing gigs as a DJ.

Music Technology and Sound Engineering course Modules include Music Theory and Music Composition. On the more technical side students can expect to study Modules in Computer Programming and Computer Music, Audio Editing Software, and Immersive Audio Techniques.

Gaining employment as a Sound Engineer can be quite challenging. Many Graduates go on to pursue careers as self-employed Sound Engineers. They can be found operating their own small recording studios, while others travel to different venues and are responsible for setting up microphones and speakers etc. to optimize the sound quality.

Course options in this sector include:

Maynooth (NUIM). Study Music Technology via Arts **(MH101)** Major/ Minor combinations available with different subjects.

University of Limerick (UL) BSc Music Media and Performance Technology **(LM114).**

TUS Limerick. BSc Music Production and Technology **(US808)** Level 8 and **(US703)** at Level 7.

TUS Athlone Campus. BSc Music and Sound Engineering **(US809)** Level 8 and **(US704)** at Level 7.

Dundalk IT. BA Audio and Music Production **(DK865)** Level 8 and **(DK768)** at level 7.

Dun Laoghaire Institute of Art, Design and Technology (IATD). BA Honours Creative Music Production **(DL838).** A Portfolio is required.

Ballyfermot College of Further Education is well known for options in Music Technology. These options are not part of the **CAO** system with direct application being made to the college. Applicants must provide evidence of their experience as well as samples of recordings they have made by submitting a Portfolio. The qualification provided is a QQI Level 5 in Sound Production with progression routes for successful students to a BTEC National Higher Diploma in Music Production. This qualification is compatible to a Higher Certificate Level 6 and has links to further Studies.

It is advised to liaise with Ballyfermot College of Further Education regarding these progression routes.

Pulse College in Dublin provides a range of courses up to and including Degree Level in the areas of Audio, Sound Engineering and Music Technology. Students apply directly to the college. Please note this is a private college and as such is not part of the Government free fees initiative.

Music Performance:

Some students buck the trend and decide to pursue a career as a Professional Musician. It is not necessary to study Music in college to become a Professional Musician. Many of the well-known performers of today honed their skills busking and playing small venues, before making it on the bigger stage, or perhaps they formed their band through meeting like-minded people at college. Many of our talented musicians have the musical gene passed down from long traditions in their family lineage. Even for these people setting up a successful band can be challenging and competitive.

Music Performance Course Options Include:

The very popular **BIMM** course through **TUD (TU961).**

MTU's Popular Music Degree **(MT937)** offers specialisms in several instruments.

DCU (DC014) offers a specialist Degree in Jazz and Contemporary Performance.

For those who have a love for Traditional Irish Music **UL's** BA in Irish Music **(LM131)** is the go-to choice.

There are a number of other music courses available, with options to study general music or combining Music with another Subject via the BA route.

Some BA options include:

UCD Joint Major in Music plus One other Subject **(DN520)** and Music, Film and Drama via **(DN530)**.

DCU Joint Honours in Music plus One other Subject **(DC009)**.

NUIM BMus **(MH103)**, or via BA **(MH101)**.

Trinity Single Honours in Music or Joint Honours in a variety of Subject choices **(TR002)**.

University of Galway BA of Music Joint Honours **(GY130)**.

UCC BMus **(CK104)** or via BA **(CK101 and CK108)**.

UL offers a BA in Music and Dance **(LM002)**, BA in Voice **(LM134)** and BA in World Music **(LM135)**.

Mary Immaculate College in Limerick offers Music through their BA **(MI002).**

Our Technological Universities also offer Degrees in music including:

MTU is the home for the renowned **Cork School of Music** and they offer a BA in Music **(MT936)** and a BA in Musical Theatre **(MT938)**.

SETU Waterford offers a BA in Music **(SE206).**

Dundalk IT offers Music Performance & Technologies **(DK892)** at Level 8 and their Degree in Musical Theatre at Level 7 **(DK771)**.

As part of the application process for several of the above-mentioned courses applicants must partake in various Assessments including an Audition, Test and Interview or a combination of these. Where a student completes these Assessments, entry to the course is based on a combination of Leaving Certificate points and points accumulated from the Assessment. Students are urged to complete their own research in order to be fully prepared for such Assessments.

The Music Archetype:

> *"They used to sit and speculate, upon their son's career,*
> *a Doctor or a Lawyer or a Civil Engineer,*
> *My parents and my lecturers could never understand,*
> *why I gave it up for Music and the free, electric band."*
>
> ***Albert Hammond***

For the Musician expression is the core. Just because you haven't gone platinum does not mean that you haven't been successful. On the contrary, Musicians bring so much to the world. Their performances are often spine-tingling, and they seem to have the ability to raise our spirits to higher levels. Music lovers often form small groups for Jamming Sessions, with some progressing onto live gigs and mixing and editing their own music via the latest creative audio technologies.

Gardener defines this intelligence as Musical, Rhythmic and Harmonic and it is easy to see the attraction of these activities for the Music minds. Most seem happy just to be involved in an industry that has been turned on its head with the advent of the Internet and Computerised Music.

Indeed, Music is also known for its therapeutic qualities and a small number of people go on to study Music Therapy at Post Graduate level and make it a career option.

As for artistic proponents – One letter and One number – **U** and **2.**

There are too many more to list.

Chapter Eleven

Art and Design

There are a variety of career options within the Art and Design Sector. A student showing interest in these areas will normally have a good idea of the specific creative area that they wish to pursue, perhaps having followed it as a hobby or having done some short courses or workshops in their chosen field. However, there are a large number of careers within this sector that students may not know or understand. In this Chapter we will explore Art and Design based careers. But before we talk about all of the wonderful courses we must first discuss Portfolios, as these Portfolios play a very important part in the application process for the vast majority of Art and Design Courses.

Portfolio and Application Process:

A student researching an Art and Design course will often see a course requiring, as an example, # 867 points. The symbol # means that entry to the specific course is based on a combination of Leaving Certificate Points, plus the Points accumulated from the presentation of a Portfolio. In general, each Portfolio is scored out of 600 points; students must get a minimum of 240 points from the Portfolio Assessment to be even considered for a place on their chosen course..

> In the example given, if an applicant receives 400 as a score for their Portfolio; they would need the balance of 467 from their Leaving Certificate points.

Each applicant must research the exact requirements, and deadlines of the Portfolio presentation, and the breakdown of points awarded. **This differs from college to college and from course to course.** Many of the colleges providing Art and Design courses facilitate workshops for prospective students during the summer between 5th and 6th year, and they also run Transition Year (TY) programs.

Due to the complexity and the need to submit the highest standard Portfolio possible, we advise students to have most of their Portfolio work completed prior to starting back to school in September of 6th year.

Some students may decide to take a Gap Year to work on their Portfolio and possibly attend a Portfolio Preparation PLC in one of the Colleges of Further Education. The Gorey School of Art is a popular choice for students from all over the country. Coláiste Dhúlaigh in Dublin also have a popular option. There are a number of private tutors facilitating workshops to support students in the preparation of their Portfolio.

Please note that entry to courses in **The National College of Art and Design (NCAD)** is purely based on the assessment of a Portfolio. There are no points awarded from the Leaving Certificate Exam. However, students must present with 2 x H5 plus 4 x O6/H7 including: Irish, English, Maths and a Third Language, or Art, or Design and Communication Graphics (DCG).

The application procedure for Art and Design Courses:

The application process includes making a **CAO** Application prior to February 1st. Many of these courses are referred to as ***Restricted Courses*** and the strict deadline for application is the 1st of February. Applicants must either physically present or digitally submit a Portfolio for assessment before the deadline set by the college. Portfolio results are available prior to June and earlier in some cases. Offers are made available as normal through the **CAO** in August.

Important Note: When reviewing the following career areas and related courses, please note that in the vast majority of cases a Portfolio will be required.

Graphic Design / Visual Communication:

Graphic Designers use their creative skills, including free hand and computer aided drawing, to create and design a range of images. They use differing texts and colours for their designs which we see every day in advertising, magazines, book covers, labels and packaging etc. They prepare the layout and templates for advertising campaigns including the positioning of text, what images to use and what colours and style are appropriate to the message being portrayed. They also create and design business logos and are often the creative forces behind the visual content used on a Company's website. In their work they use design software such as Adobe Creative, In-Design and Quark Express to create impressive designs that tell stories to their intended audience.

Courses in Graphic Design and Visual Communication include:

National College of Art and Design (NCAD). Common Entry Art and Design **(AD101)** with a specialism available after Year One or enter directly into Graphic Design/Moving Image Design via **(AD102).**

Dun Laoghaire Institute of Art, Design and Technology (IATD). Graphic Design **(DL826).**

Limerick School of Art and Design (LSAD), part of **TUS** Limerick. Common Entry Art and Design **(US800)** - specialism available after Year One.

TUS Athlone Campus. Graphic Design and Digital Art Level 8 (US806) and Graphic Design **(US700)** Level 7 .

MTU Crawford College of Art and Design, Cork. Visual Communications **(MT823)**.

TUD Grangegorman Campus. Visual Communication **(TU973).**

ATU Galway. Level 7 Design Common Entry **(AU519)** specialism into Graphic Design.

SETU Waterford. Design & Visual Communications **(SE201)**, and **SETU** Wexford: Visual Communications and Design **(SE204).**

Animation

Animators bring Stories, Films and Video Games to life. Their imagination and skill has transfixed children and adults all over the world with such creations as Wolfwalkers, Doc McStuffins, Toy Story and Avatar etc. Indeed Ireland is well known for its global successes in the area of Animation. In recent years Irish Companies have been to the fore in achieving Oscar nominations and wins. While some animators continue to work purely in the traditional format, creating characters and story boards by hand, it is now a more technical based career where computer generated images are used, allowing for faster and more elaborate special effects to be included.

Some courses in Animation include:

NCAD. Common Entry Art and Design **(AD101)**, with specialism available after Year One into an option in Illustration, focusing more on the drawing side, or an option in Moving Image Design focusing more on the digital side of Animation.

IATD. The following options are available: Animation **(DL832)**, 3D Animation **(DL847)**, and Creative Computing **(DL836)**.

Limerick School of Art and Design (LSAD), part of **TUS** Limerick. Art and Design Common Entry **(US800)**, with specialism available after Year One into Animation and Motion Design.

TUS Athlone Campus. Animation and Illustration Level 8 **(US802)** and Level 7 (US778).

TUS Clonmel Campus. Digital Animation **(US805)**.

ATU Galway. Animation and Game Design **(AU617)**.

MTU Kerry. Animation, Visual Effects and Motion Design **(MT711)** Level 7.

Interior Design / Interior Architecture:

Interior Designers are all about optimizing the aesthetics of an interior space. Issues for the Interior Designer include what does the space look like? Is it appealing to the eye? In comparison the **Interior Architect** is more concerned about the functionality of the interior space and how the space works from a user's perspective. However, there is definitely a cross over between the two roles, with each carrying out a lot of similar tasks during the course of their work.

Many of these Interior Design Professionals will see themselves in self-employed roles seeking contracts or completing tenders to work on a wide variety of Design projects. Examples of these contracts could include the design or renovation of the interior space of a hotel, office building, or even a private residence.

They use vision boards either created by hand or digitally to bring together the concepts that they propose for the interior space in question. These vision boards include the use of colours, fabrics, wood and metals. Their suggestions might also suggest demolition of interior walls to open up the space and make it more open plan and flowing. Interior Designers/Architects work closely with Professionals from the construction industry, including Architects, Builders, Carpenters, Painters and Quantity Surveyors. They always have to keep in mind the budget allowed for the work and be creative in the materials they use while ensuring they follow the brief of their client.

Options to study Interior Architecture/Design include:

LSAD part of **TUS** Limerick. Art and Design Common Entry **(US800)**, with specialism available after Year One into Interior Design or enter directly via Interior Design **(US811).**

TUD Grangegorman Campus. Interior Design **(TU975)** entry on to this course requires a Portfolio.

ATU Galway. Interior Design **(AU622)**.

ATU Sligo. Interior Architecture Level 8 (AU926) and Level 7 **(AU820).**

MTU Bishopstown Campus. Interior Architecture at Level 8 **(MT860)** and Level 7 **(MT760).**

Fashion Design:

An aspiring Fashion Designer must be brave; it is a career that calls for persistence, determination and a burning desire to succeed. From designing Haute Couture fashion to ready to wear High Street fashion; these Designers always have to be on the top of their game.

They use their artistic and technical skills to envisage and create new pieces of clothing and accessories that will wow their intended customers. Designing clothing which is sustainability has become a very important part of their work. They love being in their design studio sketching by hand, cutting patterns and draping luxurious materials onto mannequins or models. They visit fashion shows and fairs to gather ideas and to keep abreast as to what is happening in the fashion world.

Ireland has a good reputation in this industry with people such as Kate Middleton, Lady Gaga, Taylor Swift, and Michelle Obama wearing original designs by Irish Fashion Designers. Gaining experience and building a Portfolio of work is the key in this competitive and demanding world particularly as you start out in your career.

To qualify in Ireland the options include:

NCAD. Common Entry Art and Design **(AD101)** with a specialism available after Year One or entry directly via Fashion Design **(AD211)**.

LSAD. Art and Design Common Entry **(US800)**, with specialism available after Year One into Fashion Design.

ATU Galway. Level 7 Design Common Entry **(AU519)** specialism into Textile and Fashion Design or enter directly into Textile and Fashion Design at Level 8 **(AU621)**.

ATU Letterkenny. Level 7 in Fashion Design and Promotion **(AU232)**.

Griffith College Dublin offers a Level 8 option **(GC464)** and a Level 7 option **(GC495)** in Fashion Design.

Grafton Academy of Fashion Design have a range of courses in fashion design and related areas from a 3 year diploma to a 1 month intensive course in sewing. This college is non **CAO** and students apply directly to Grafton Academy.

Both Griffith College and the **Grafton Academy** are **fee paying** colleges.

Visual Merchandising and Display:

The majority of Visual Merchandisers work in the retail sector, creating, designing, and managing both window displays, and in store displays for the likes of fashion, household and homeware products. Many of the big chain retail stores such as H&M, Penny's, Dunne's Stores for example, will have a central theme design that must be copied in all the stores right around the country/world. It is the job of the Visual Merchandiser to make sure this happens, but of course, they can add their ***own twist*** to each display. They are responsible for the ***image*** of the store to make it appealing for customers to visit. These Visual Merchandisers are normally very busy during changes of season, designing and creating window and instore displays reflective of the time of year, for example Christmas and Easter.

An eye for detail, good spatial awareness and interest in ever changing fashion trends and brands would be helpful for anyone thinking about this role.

Courses in Visual Merchandising and Display include:

TUD Grangegorman Campus. Level 7 option is the best known course **(TU795).**

ATU Letterkenny. Level 7 in Fashion Design and Promotion **(AU232)** will also provide qualification to work in this area.

Portobello Institute (Private College). BA (Honours) Fashion Buying and Merchandising. Apply directly to Portobello. Award from **London Metropolitan University.**

Fashion Buying:

Often students who have a keen interest in fashion trends, but who are not keen to work in the Design field, show a leaning towards the area of Fashion Buying. Many students who have part time retail jobs in large fashion retailers might have had some exposure to what Fashion Buying involves.

At the moment the options to qualify in Fashion Buying include:

Portobello Institute (Fee Paying College). BA Honours in Fashion Buying and Merchandising. Apply directly to Portobello. Award from **London Metropolitan University.**

SETU Waterford. Fashion Buying and Retail Management at Level 7 **(SE419).**

Crumlin College of Further Education. QQI Level 5 in Fashion Buying and Merchandising is a very popular option for students wishing to find out more about this area.

Alternatively students will progress to Post Graduate Studies into MSc Fashion Buying and Management with **TUD**, or other options in the **UK.**

Fine Art, Sculpture, Painting, and Print:

I want to be an Artist. These six words can often inspire fear in parents as they bring up images of their loved one struggling to find a job in the real world of paying bills and having financial security. However, for young people who love the creative process, this is often the only path they can realistically see themselves pursuing. Through their ability to think outside the box and see things in three-dimensional form, they gift us with outstanding works of art across a number of disciplines. The form of each piece is unique and covers a huge range of artwork. These pieces can include abstract paintings, a sculpture, or perhaps a unique piece of jewellery to pass down through the generations.

Not only are their pieces of work unique, but Artists themselves are often unique and original in the way they present themselves to the world. They long to have an exhibition of their work and while the financial rewards may take time to come, they get great satisfaction from people admiring and appreciating their work. Because of the nature of their work, most Artists will work for themselves from their own studio space. Very often in order to make enough money they will diversify into Design Based Crafts, making the likes of Jewellery, Ceramics, Glass or Pottery.

Many of these Artists confess to not being blessed with strong Business skills, and it is common for some Artists to come together to work collaboratively in a joint studio with other Artists.

There are a number of Fine Art course options including:

NCAD. (AD104) Common Entry Fine Art and Applied Art with specialisms in Fine Art, Media, Painting, Print, Sculpture or Applied Art, Ceramics and Glass, or Textile Art and Artefact. (AD101) Common Entry Art and Design, with specialism available into: Print, Media, Sculpture, Painting or Textile and Surface Design, and Jewellery and Objects. Or direct Entry to Textiles, Jewellery and Objects with (AD103).

IADT. Art **(DL827).**

LSAD TUS Limerick. Art and Design Common Entry **(US800)**, with specialism available into: Painting, Print, Sculpture, and Ceramics.

MTU Crawford College of Art and Design, Cork. Contemporary Art, Ceramics, Glass and Textiles **(MT820)**, Fine Art **(MT821)**.

TUD, Grangegorman Campus. Fine Art **(TU974)** or Visual Art (Sherkin Island) **(TU977).**

ATU Sligo. Fine Art at level 8 **(AU928)** and Level 7 **(AU822).**

SETU Wexford. Art at Level 8 **(SE207)** and Level 7 **(SE211).**

During the course of their work some Artists will find themselves facilitating art interventions with community groups, perhaps working with people with disability, acquired brain injury or Alzheimer's. If they find this work fulfilling they can take it a step further by completing the **MA** in Art Therapy with **MTU/Crawford College** in Cork or a MA Art, Psyche and the Creative Imagination at **TUS** Limerick. **Please note** these courses do not qualify the individual as a **Counsellor/Psychotherapist** (see section on Psychology and Social Sciences).

Photography:

Have you ever imagined yourself as a photographer on a professional shoot? A chance to work with the stars of Fashion, Music or Sports. If you are lucky enough to have the opportunity to work in this arena, then you will have reached the pinnacle of the Photography Profession. On the other hand, you have gained employment as a Press photographer with one of the major media outlets, and if so, you are in a niche group. You bring the news into our homes by the images you capture at sporting events, musical festivals, and political events and unfortunately, too often war and human suffering.

The majority of Photographers, however, will be self-employed, setting up their own studio. They make their livelihood from social events such as weddings and school and college graduations. Not only are they charged with getting a perfect shot by using the correct lighting, reflectors and back drops, but they also work in their dark rooms using chemicals and equipment to produce physical photographic prints. While a lot of photographs are now digitized, the use of dark rooms is still part of the work. So, while Photography can be a creative area to work in, it is definitely a profession that includes its fair share of technical aspects.

Courses in Photography include:

IADT Photography and Visual Media **(DL833)**.

TUD Grangegorman Campus. Photography **(TU976)**.

MTU Cork Campus. Photography with New Media **(MT822).**

Griffith College Dublin (Private College). Level 7 in Photographic Media. Apply directly to Griffith College.

Students will also find Photography Modules in courses including Graphic Design, Visual Communication, and TV and Film Courses.

Product and Industrial Design:

Product Designers think visually and they like first-hand problem solving. Product design is associated with students who enjoy DCG, Technology, Engineering, or Art and those who have an innovative and entrepreneurial mind-set. They use their expertise to bring new designs into the world from ergonomically designed office chairs to sustainable and environmentally friendly household appliances and from medical devices to children's toys.

Initially Product Designers work on the process of getting their ideas to the prototype stage. They consider what materials are best used to optimize the product quality and ensure all safety measures are adhered to in the design. They work with manufacturing companies to ensure that their designs are followed throughout the manufacturing process. These designers are not only working on new products but coming up with ways to improve existing products to keep them up to

date with our evolving and technology-based world.
Courses focus on the full process of product design including generating the ideas, the initial design, the technical aspects of product design and of course the business side, in particular marketing.

Course options in Product and Industrial design include:

NCAD: Common Entry Art and Design **(AD101)** with a specialism in Product Design OR direct entry via Product Design **(AD212).**

TUD Grangegorman Campus: Product Design **(TU811)** with an emphasis on Engineering.

UL: Product Design and Technology **(LM076).**

NUIM: Product Design and Innovation **(MH305)**.

SETU Carlow: Level 8 Product Design and Innovation **(SE202)** or Industrial Design Level 7 **(SE209).**

Furniture Design:

Students who like Woodwork at Junior Cert Level and Construction Studies at Leaving Cert Level, along with other subjects such as DCG or Art, are often drawn to Furniture Design. They want to be the creative force and designer of bespoke furniture pieces. They understand natural and manmade materials and how these can be used to create pieces of furniture. They may see a new coffee table or chair as not just a piece of furniture, but as a work of art. They envisage themselves as the designer behind the next state of the art contemporary kitchen, or perhaps the originator of a design that will be sold across the country in major furniture outlets. Not only do they want to design one off pieces, they also quite enjoy being first-hand in the making of it.

Courses in Furniture Design include:

ATU Galway run their renowned courses in Furniture Design between their campuses in Connemara and Galway City. Furniture Design and Manufacturing **(AU681)**. Furniture Making and Technology **(AU683).** Furniture Making and Architectural Woodworking **(AU682)**.

TUD Grangegorman Campus. Interior & Furniture Design **(TU975),** entry to this course requires a Portfolio. Another option is Sustainable Timber Technology at **TUD** Bolton Street **(TU838)** Level 7. This course covers areas including, but not limited to, Furniture Design, Joinery, the Science of Wood, and the Business side of Timber Production.

There a number of **QQI** Level 5 **PLC** in the area of Furniture Making and Woodworking in Colleges of Further Education right around the country. These courses can often be a good starting point for anyone interested in the area of furniture design and manufacturing

Culinary Arts:

We also include cooking as one of the creative careers. Since the explosion of celebrity chefs and food programmes we have found that the culinary arts are prevalent and employable all over the world. Master Chef Programmes being beamed into our living rooms seem to have added a completely new and exciting dimension to working with food. Because of this, there has never been such a demand for high standard cuisine served to the consumer in an aesthetically appealing manner. The plate must be ***Instagram Ready.***

Cooking tasty food is only part of the role, it is now an art form in the presentation and service of food. Depending on where you work will really determine the creative input you have as a Culinary Artist. For some this input can be quite limited, especially in restaurants and hotels where there is an established approach to menu planning. In another scenario a newly qualified Chef might be mentored by the Head Chef in a Michelin Star Restaurant.

Some others in this profession will go it alone and work on designing specialty cakes (Confectionery), or developing new Artisan foods such as Fermented Foods, Protein Rich Foods or Vegan and Vegetarian options. Often the motivation to go it alone comes from the challenge of continuously producing high quality meals in what can be a pressurized workplace at times.

Courses to Consider for Qualification

TUD Grangegorman Campus. Culinary Arts Level 8 **(TU942),** Culinary Entrepreneurship **(TU943)** Level 8, Culinary Science **(TU944)** Level 8, or Baking and Pastry Arts Management **(TU741)** Level 7.

TUD Tallaght Campus. Culinary Arts **(TU742)** Level 7 and Level 6 **(TU031).**

Dundalk I.T. Culinary Arts Level 7 (DK753).

ATU Galway. Gastronomy Science and Food Innovation Level 8 **(AU631)**, and a Level 6 option in Culinary Arts, Professional Chef **(AU429)**.

SETU Waterford. Culinary Arts at Level 8 **(SE923)** and a Level 6 option **(SE938).**

MTU Cork. BBS in Culinary Arts at Level 7 **(MT555)** and a Level 6 option in Culinary Studies (MT655).

There are also a number of Apprenticeship options to train as a Chef. See **www.apprenticeship.ie** for further information about this ***earn while you learn*** approach.

Other options in the creative areas include the careers of Beauty Therapy, Hairdressing and Barbering. There are a number of **PLC** courses at **QQI** Level 5 and 6 available in these areas. These courses are normally the starting point for anybody interested in pursuing one of these careers.

There are now many hairdressing salons providing **SOLAS** approved apprenticeships in Hairdressing. See **www.apprenticeship.ie** for further information about this ***earn while you learn*** approach. Once the individual has finished their initial training there are a host of training courses and specialized areas to progress into.

The Creative Archetype:

When asked about careers in the creative sector, most of our clients answer with the statement: ***I can't draw.*** Some take this even further by emphasising the fact that they can't even draw a straight line. Unfortunately, this is typical of so many people. While this is what they experience in their own mind, in truth we know that every human being is born creative. Sadly because of an education system that is almost exclusively dominated by left brain logical teaching methods, the gift that is their natural 'birth right' has been shut down effectively by the age of ten. If only they knew that this negative step could be reversed, then we might live in a much more inspiring and beautiful world.

Thankfully, however, a percentage of people do manage to resist the onslaught on their Creative – Musical – Visual and Spatial Intelligence and go on to pursue further studies in the creative areas. Flare, exuberance and a passion for the finer things in life, define the Creative Archetype. This person loves to paint, draw and sculpt new designs and they have a strong desire to bring something new into the world of beauty and aesthetics.

Careers in Art and Design are often a labour of love, and in a lot of cases Artists do not have a regular defined job in the normal sense of the word. This doesn't seem to deter the budding Artist or Designer in the least however, as they cannot envision any other way of living their life.

Chapter Twelve

Science

Science remains a popular choice for many Leaving Certificate students. There are a huge number of Degree options to choose from and narrowing down these choices can be a difficult task. One thing that all Science courses have in common however, is a first year that always includes the study of these Core Modules: Biology, Chemistry, Physics, Maths and Information Technology (I.T.). It's no surprise then that we often get calls from distressed first years floundering with this difficult mix. The main reason for this is that while many students like Science and have taken a Science Subject among their Leaving Certificate choices, the vast majority have taken Biology only. In many cases if students haven't chosen a second Science Subject in their Leaving Certificate mix, they often struggle with the complexities of University Chemistry and Physics. Indeed, over the years we have received many calls from students that find it hard to keep up with the demands of Maths in their Science course also.

We don't want to be too negative about studying Science, however we do caution about the first-year mix, and prospective students need to consider this as part of their decision-making process. The good news is that having completed first year successfully, subsequent years can be much more interesting as you journey into your chosen specialist field.

Common Entry Science:

In Ireland today most colleges offer a Common Entry Science Degree. In first year, students engage with all of the fundamentals of Biology, Chemistry etc. as mentioned previously. Following a core first year students can then decide to opt for a range of specialist topics which can be studied up to and including their final year.

The range of specialisms on offer can be mind boggling, none more so than UCD Science (DN200) which has a staggering twenty-seven different Degree options from the same first year entry (See UCD webpage to explore the Multiple Streams option). These twenty-seven Degree options are subdivided into Biological and Biomedical, Chemical, Earth and Environmental, Mathematical, Physics and Education streams.

If selecting Science at Trinity one must commit to a specific stream on the CAO application, for example Biological and Biomedical (TR060) or Chemical Sciences (TR061). Trinity is home to Ireland's only Undergraduate Degree in both Immunology and Human Genetics.

All the other Universities / Technological Universities offer Common Entry Sciences as an option and students should check the respective Degree specialisms before choosing which college they would like to study Science in. Some of the Technological Universities, including MTU, ATU and SETU, offer common entry Degree options at both Level 8 and Level 7.

Food Science:

Food Science is normally studied as an entry level Degree and is not offered as an option within Common Entry Science in most cases. Among the most popular courses in Ireland are Food Science at UCD (DN261) and UCC (CK505), while Nutraceuticals in Health and Nutrition is a good option at TUD (TU882). Because the food industry is so big in Ireland there is a strong demand for Food Science Graduates at all times.

Medical Laboratory Technician:

To work as a Medical Laboratory Technician in one of Ireland's hospitals, one must have completed one of only three recognised Degree courses currently offered in this country. These courses are Biomedical Science at TUD (TU867), Biomedical Science at MTU Cork Campus (MT871), offered jointly by MTU and UCC, and Medical Science ATU (AU671) Galway City Campus. As demand is high for places on these courses, points tend to be high at around 500 or better.

Health Sciences:

There are a range of other Biomedical Science Degrees at other Universities, many of which are high points. While these Degrees are excellent, they do not lead to qualification as a Medical Laboratory Technician. Most of the Graduates from these Degrees find their way into research positions with large Pharmaceutical Companies, while others often apply for Post Graduate courses such as Graduate Medicine. Courses include:

University College Cork. Medical & Health Science **(CK707)**.

Trinity College. Human Health and Disease **(TR056)**.

University College Dublin. Biomedical Health & Life Science **(DN440).**

Royal College of Surgeons (RCSI). Advanced Therapeutics Technology **(RC006).**

University of Galway. Biomedical Science **(GY303).**

Points requirements for these courses can be high and normally exceed 500 points minimum (in some cases they exceed 550).

Pharmaceutical Sciences:

Over two thirds of the world's top Pharmaceutical Companies have manufacturing/research bases in Ireland. Demand for Chemistry and Pharmaceutical Sciences Graduates is continually strong among those Companies. Pharma Companies are often seen as Companies that pay the best salaries and they all provide excellent opportunities for career growth and development. Pharmaceutical Companies tend to gather around most of our major towns and cities.

For those who love Chemistry and would like to go directly into a

Chemistry Degree there are some very good options available. Chemical Pharmaceutical Science at **DCU (DC163)** is very strong and covers all the main topics in great detail. For lower point options there is Pharmaceutical Science at **SETU** Waterford **(SE504)** or Chemical and Pharmaceutical Science at **ATU (AU670)** Galway.

Forensic Science:

Chemistry is also very important for Forensic Sciences. The Forensic Scientist is primarily involved in analysing evidence taken from a crime scene. Students often make the mistake of thinking they will be out at crime scenes searching for and collecting evidence. This is not the case as this role is performed by highly trained members of An Garda Siochána (Technical Bureau). Most of the analysis carried out in Ireland is at the state sponsored Forensics Ireland Laboratory based in the Phoenix Park.

There are a number of specialist Forensic Science courses available through the CAO. These include:

UCC Common Entry Science **(CK402)**: Chemical and Forensic Pathway.

TUS Limerick (US863): Pharmaceutical and Forensic Analysis.

TUD Grangegorman (TU851): Forensic and Environmental Chemistry.

TUD Tallaght Campus. DNA and Forensic Science, Level 7 and 8 Entry Routes **(TU864** and **TU752).**

Please note a full Honours Degree in Forensic Science is not an absolute must when it comes to applying to Forensics Ireland. For the post of Analyst, the minimum academic qualification is a level 7 qualification in an appropriate Science Subject. For the post of Scientist, the minimum academic qualification is an Honours Degree (level 8), normally in Chemistry, Analytical Science or an appropriate Biological Subject such as Biochemistry, Biology or Molecular Biology, or an equivalent qualification. A formal qualification in Forensic Science is not required as all new staff members will be fully trained on the job.

Physics Degrees:

Physics as a Science can be studied through General Science or as a stand-alone Degree. For a student that is interested in Astronomy and Space Science then a Physics Degree normally caters for this interesting Subject. **Maynooth University (MH204) Trinity College (TR063)** and **UCD (DN200)** are well known for their Space Science options. Mind you, the opportunities that exist for Space Science Graduates around the country are understandably limited, as there is little or no Space Science related industry in Ireland. Consequently, many Physics Graduates go on to further studies with a view to gaining employment in research roles.

Physics courses are mathematical by nature and as such most successful Graduates have a strong ability in Maths. Theoretical Physics at Trinity (TR035) is two thirds Maths and one third Physics in first year before evening out into an equal ratio for subsequent years.

What do Scientists do?

As you can imagine Scientists play a very important role in our world today. From the Microbiologist at a large hospital to the Forensic Scientist analysing evidence taken from a crime scene, the career opportunities open to a well-qualified Scientist are numerous.

To help you with your research we divide Science careers into two broad categories.

Quality Assurance and Research:

Quality Assurance is a vital part of ensuring that the foodstuffs and medicines we consume on a daily basis are safe for human consumption. When a newborn baby is given its first bottle of Infant Milk, we must be sure that the product contains no unwanted bacteria that would upset the baby's digestive system. The formulation on such a product should also be a perfect blend of vitamins, minerals and proteins to give the baby the perfect head start. Similarly with pharmaceutical drugs the active ingredients must be exactly as approved by the relevant controlling authorities such as the **F.D.A.**. No chances can be taken with incorrect formulations, as mistakes at this stage can have very serious consequences. This is where Quality Assurance plays a critical role, and many new Science Graduates begin their career in this field. Many go on to have rewarding careers in Quality Engineering or in **QA Management.**

Science Researchers:

These scientists play a hugely important role in the development of medicines across the globe. When Alexander Fleming invented Penicillin nearly one hundred years ago few could have imagined the impact that this invention would have on the world of medicine. Fast forward one hundred years and on this occasion the world needed a major breakthrough to combat the Covid 19 Pandemic. This time it was Tess Lambe, an Irish Science Professor at Oxford University, who was accredited with being one of the first researchers to produce an effective Covid vaccine, the AstraZeneca D1222.

A career as a Science Researcher can often require some Post Graduate studies beyond the traditional Level 8 Honours Degree. For those aspiring to work in the growing Biomedical Research areas then a Master's Degree in, for example, Neuroscience or Immunology are popular choices. Indeed, many experienced researchers take the final academic steps into PhD Doctorate Studies and use this specialist knowledge to contribute to leading edge research teams across the Globe.

If you would like to transform the future of healthcare by using the power of Science, then a career as an R&D Scientist might be just the thing for you.

The Scientist Archetype:

Carrying out investigations and a quest to know how this world of ours is put together motivates the Science archetype. Scientists explore the core of our being from neural pathways to nano technologies. This career covers a broad range of issues, including Biomedical, Biological, Chemical and Pharmacological systems.

The scientist's precision and accuracy often leads them into inspectorate roles, crucial during war time, and subsequently refined into modern day Quality Assurance. Quality Assurance is a critical role in the huge multi-national manufacturing sector. For a new Graduate there are plenty of opportunities to get their first **QA Inspector** role in either a food or pharmaceutical company. Quality Assurance offers many different career paths that can lead right up to a senior management position such as Quality Assurance Manager. There are many steps along the route including Team Leader, Validation Technician,

Quality Engineer, Technical Writer, and Documentation Controller to name but a few. The majority of Science Graduates pursue roles such as these.
Research is the Mecca for budding Scientists. They love the challenge of finding answers and cures to humanity's problems such as malaria and cancer. Microbiologists and Biotechnologists on the other hand, hunt down super resistant bugs such as MRSA in hospitals, and they also try to stay ahead of nature with the development of evermore complex compounds and antibiotics.

People with high levels of this intelligence, don't always need other people around them. Because sometimes Researchers in Science often spend extended periods working on their own, a sense of intrapersonal introversion is often well suited to that role.
Academically strong, the skilled Scientist will have studied Biology and most importantly Chemistry. Chemistry explores the building blocks of the universe, and with this knowledge, Scientists have helped to shape the modern world by their introduction of everyday materials such as polymers and polyester. While Physics (including the study of Astronomy and Space Science) also forms part of the Science family, people with strong mathematical ability are more likely to plump for careers as Nuclear or Astro Physicists.

Chapter Thirteen

Natural Sciences

Environmental Studies:

Environmental Science concerns itself with the impact of human activity on the environment, and Environmental Scientists use Chemistry and Biology to analyse and interpret this impact. They work in the field gathering samples and observational data but also work in the Laboratory conducting testing and analysis. For example, they often analyse water and soil for pollutants caused by industry and agriculture. They will test water, soil or air samples to find the type, concentration and source of the pollution. The Environmental Scientist will then undertake a rigorous assessment to identify if that contaminant source has the potential to affect or harm the environment. In their work they will build conceptual models to identify the source of contaminant and its potential to spread and impact its surroundings. Environmental Scientists have to write detailed scientific reports on their findings and often have to communicate these to many groups or individuals. A portion of their work will be monitoring and advising manufacturing industries on the safe disposal of waste product and the prevention of environmental damage. Anyone considering this career should have a keen interest in Chemistry.

Well known courses in this area include:

Biological, Environment and Geological Studies at **UCC (CK404)** has a strong reputation over a number of years and points are highest here at 500+. Both **University of Limerick (LM066)**, and **University of Galway (GY308)** offer Degrees in the 400 to 450 points range. **Trinity's** Biological Science Streams **(TR060)**

allow students to specialise into Environmental Science in Year Three. Points are in the high 500's. **ATU** Sligo offers Environmental Science options at both Level 8 **(AU966)** and Level 7 **(AU855)**, with points here in the 300 range.

Environmental Sustainability:

There are a range of new Environmental Sustainability courses being offered by Universities in Ireland. These courses tend to focus on the broader issues facing the planet, as opposed to the traditional Science-based approach as described previously.

New courses at UCD (DC240) Sustainability, and DCU (DC294) Climate and Environmental Sustainability, offer a range of pathways and learning styles relating to the urgent issue of Global Warming. Points for these courses are normally in the 475 – 525 regions. TUD (TU835) also offers and excellent Degree in Environmental Management with points lower and in the mid 300's.

Earth and Ocean Sciences:

A small percentage of students have a strong interest in studying all aspects of our earth, oceans and atmosphere. Through studying Earth and Ocean Sciences they have the opportunity to learn about the processes that shape the earth. This fascinating study area includes modules on how the earth works, the hazards of earthquakes and volcanoes and much more. Subjects studied include all of the basic Sciences as well as specialist Modules such as: Mineral and Fuel Deposits, Geology and Geobiology, Environmental Geology, Oceanography and Palaeontology.

As an Earth and Ocean Scientist you will be well placed to advise companies and organisations on how to best manage the resources and the environment we live in. Many Graduates find themselves pursuing Post Graduate Study to enhance their career prospects as Research Assistants.

University of Galway's offers the BSc Earth and Ocean Sciences **(GY314)** with reasonable points in the low 400's. Students can also access Earth Ocean Science via General Science pathway **(GY301)**.

Again the BSc Biological Environmental and Geological Science (previously referred to as the BEES) in UCC give relevant modules in the area of Earth Ocean Sciences. Geoscience **(TR062)** at Trinity and general Science **(DN200)** at UCD specialising into Geology also have relevant modules.

Marine Biologists:

Marine Biologists study microorganisms, plant and animal life in the ocean and on the shoreline. They conduct research in the laboratory and at sea on research ships. They analyse and interpret data from remote sensing aids. They are interested in the processes of how marine organisms adapt to their environment and interact with it. They may also study the effects of pollution and industrial activity on the oceans and the levels of stocks of particular fish species.

These people are fascinated by the existence of bacteria, plankton, algae, larvae and worms. They will use techniques including trawling with plankton nets to collect and study and record these marine specimens. In more recent times Marine Biologists have been monitoring the effects of micro plastics in our oceans.

Employment opportunities for Graduates are quite limited. Many students engage in Post Graduate Studies to avail of employment. There are some opportunities available within the Marine Industry, particularly Fisheries, and Government Bodies such as the Environmental Protection Agency.

The BSc Marine Science at University Galway **(GY310)** is currently the only Irish University offering this Degree, and points are in the high 400s.
ATU Galway offer good options via Level 8 BSc (Honours) in Applied Freshwater and Marine Biology **(AU655)** also available at Level 7 **(AU555)** with points in the low 400s and 300s respectively.

Plant Sciences:

Horticulture is the Science and Technology of plant cultivation. In general those working in Horticulture produce young plants from seedlings, bulbs, cutting or by techniques know as grafting. Work is usually outdoors or in a controlled environment such as a greenhouse. A lot of the work is done by hand, such as planting, but will also involve the use of heavy machinery for rotavating and fertilising. A keen interest in nature and ability to work on your own with physical endurance is necessary for this career choice. You will work in all types of weather and terrain. Health and Safety is very important in this role, including the safe use of equipment, machinery and chemical sprays. This work may also involve general garden and park maintenance such as pruning shrubs and staking plants depending on the season.

There are two major types of Horticulturist.

Commercial Horticulture involves growing crops and plants for sale. Crops include fruit and vegetables, nursery stock, bedding plants as well as medicinal plants. This sector uses advanced botanical techniques such as plant propagation. You will often find Horticulturists giving advice in garden centres.

Amenity Horticulture tends to focus more on the design, installation and upkeep of specialist public parks and gardens. Professional Gardeners and Landscape Contractors are associated with this sector. Sports Turf Management and Greenkeeping are roles which are linked to Amenity Horticulture.

Landscape Design There are also professional Landscape Architects that concentrate purely on the Design aspects of these spaces. Currently there is one course in Ireland that gives a full Honours Degree qualification, and that is Landscape Architecture at **UCD (DN120).**

Plant Sciences and Botany:

One can train as a Botanist via General Science at University and then take Botany as their Major in final years. The role of a Botanist is very specialised and the main emphasis of their work is to evaluate and improve plant life. They work in Laboratories and Botanical Gardens measuring the effects of pollution on plant life and biodiversity. They may also be called upon to advice on the control of invasive species such as knotweed.

Employment opportunities are dependent on your area of expertise. They include Local Authorities, Office of Public Works (OPW), Golf Clubs, Commercial Soft Fruit Farms, Garden Centres and Nurseries.

Popular Courses include:

UCD via Agricultural Science **(DN250)**. **SETU** Waterford, Kildalton for Commercial Horticulture **(SE506)**, and National Botanical Gardens, Dublin for Amenity Horticulture **(SE507)**. There are also some QQ1 Level 5 with **Teagasc** available.

Forestry:

Trees are becoming a very important resource in the world today. Because of their proven ability to capture carbon we need to greatly increase the number of trees we grow in Ireland and the world today. As a country Ireland has a much lower acreage under trees than all of our European counterparts and this is a statistic that needs to change. Hence there has never been a better time to consider Forestry as a career.

Traditionally Foresters have been associated with working for the State Forestry organisation, **Coillte**. However there are many other roles that need the skills of this outdoor based career. The Christmas Tree industry is worth around €15 million annually while companies like Bulmers need thousands of acres to grow their apple crops. Some Forestry Graduates work for themselves in another growing sector, that of the Tree Surgeon.

To become a Forester in Ireland today the career paths are very similar to those mapped out previously for Horticulturalists. Agriculture Science at **UCD (DN250)** specialising into Forestry and **SETU** Waterford offer a Level 7 option **(SE505)**. Teagasc offer a very good practical route to qualification through its QQI Level 5/6 course in Ballyhaise, County Cavan.

Working with Animals:

Careers involving working with animals are very popular with students. Many dream of becoming a Vet. However, the entry requirements for a place on Veterinary Medicine in Ireland are consistently high. In addition to achieving high points students must also present with a H5 in Higher Chemistry and a Third Language.

If a person does not make the grade requirements for Veterinary Medicine, all is not lost; there are other possibilities when it comes to working with animals. In this section we will give a short overview of all animal related career options.

Veterinary Medicine:

Ireland's only Undergraduate Degree is offered by **UCD (DN300)**. Year on year the demand for this course outweighs the number of places available so points are normally in the high 500's. The course is of five-years duration. Undergraduate students applying through the **CAO** for this course must demonstrate that they have acquired at least 60 hours practical experience relevant to animal handling between February of Fifth Year and early July of their Leaving Certificate Year. There is criteria in place as to where you can gain this experience so students need to check the UCD Veterinary Medicine web page for details.

Note: *Early in May 2025 the then Taoiseach Simon Harris announced plans to deliver two new veterinary medicine schools in Ireland. The new veterinary medicine courses will be offered at Atlantic Technological University (ATU), and South East Technological University (SETU). At time of print course codes for these programmes were not available.*

Due to the high demand for places, many Irish students tend to look further afield to qualify. For many years **Budapest** in Hungary was the most popular destination, but latterly we are finding that more and more students are targeting **Warsaw** in Poland.

The Process of applying to these colleges normally includes some or all of the following;

Pre Entry exams in Biology/Chemistry and certain cases Physics. Students can choose between; Written Multiple Choice Questions and Interview or Oral Exam and Interview.

Fees are **€8500 to €14500** approximitely per annum along with accomodation and living expenses.Please refer to the section on 'Studying in Europe' for more details.

Veterinary Science in the UK:

Entry is very competitive with some colleges requiring H2 in Chemistry and Biology and a H2 in either Maths or Physics with H3 in two other subjects. In addition work experience is also required prior to commencing study. See specific requirements on individual college web sites. UK Colleges are quoting annual fees in the region of £9,250 Sterling per annum for Irish students Please refer to the section on 'UCAS' for application details.

Post Graduate Veterinary Medicine via UCD:

Once again a competitive process with only five places on offer each year. Graduates that are lucky enough to come through the application process must complete an additional 4 years of study at Post Graduate level.

Best Honours Degrees for entry purposes include Level 8 Honours Degree in Biological, Bioveterinary or Animal Science. For entry Graduates must sit the GAMSAT Tests as well as completing a Personal Statement.

Tip: Best advice for those wishing to studying Veterinary in Ireland, Europe or UK; Take Higher level Chemistry, Biology and Maths or Physics at Leaving Certificate Level bearing in mind that you will need a third languge to study Veterinary in Ireland.

Veterinary Nursing:

For those that care deeply for animals but may not be interested or capable of qualifying as a Vet, then Veterinary Nursing may be an option. Experienced Veterinary Nurses often play an important role in the care and welfare of animals. While the Veterinary Nurse is primarily a support role, they are often the first port of call when it comes to assessing the needs of a sick animal. As such, Veterinary Nurses play a central role in the day to day running of most Veterinary Clinics. They possess an excellent grasp of all ailments and illnesses that afflict our animal friends.

There are a number of options that lead to qualification as a Veterinary Nurse.

UCD (DN310) offers a full Level 8 Honours Degree and is very popular because of its links to the **UCD School of Veterinary Medicine.** Recent points have been in the 450 – 500 range.

There are four colleges offering Level 7 Degrees, **Dundalk IT (DK784)**, TUS Athlone **(US738)**, ATU Letterkenny **(AU271)** and **MTU** Tralee **(MT784)**. These Level 7 courses tend to average around the 400 points mark and some of them require students to have Leaving Certificate Biology.

Finally, **Cork College of Further Education** offer a two-year QQI Level 6 qualification in Veterinary Nursing and successful Graduates of this course are fully eligible for Registration as Veterinary Nurses.

Animal Science:

Animal Science is primarily the study of animals kept on Irish Farms. These animals are mainly cattle, sheep and pigs, but can include smaller animals such as poultry. Animal Science focuses on best demonstrated practices that improve the health and quality of the animal. This Science also focuses on the improvement of genetics within Ireland's animal population. While it is common for the sons and daughters of Irish farmers to study Animal Science, many students from non-farming families pursue this avenue.

Course Options for the Study of Animal Science:

Probably the best-known course for Animal Science is **(DN250)** via Agriculture Science at **UCD.** This course has a general First Year before specialising into Animal Science in Year Two (note this is just one specialism from eleven Degree options which also include Dairy Business and Equine Science).

Animal Science can also be studied via general Agriculture Science at popular courses such as **SETU (SE502), UCC (CK412)** (emphasises on dairy) or **MTU Cork (MT750)**, University of Galway **(GY322)** or **ATU**, with options at Mountbellew **(AU657)** and Letterkenny **(AU371)**.

Equestrian Science:

Equestrian Science is the study of horses. For many years the Irish Horse Industry has enjoyed an extremely strong international reputation. Whether through breeding at stud farms or via training champion race horses and show jumpers, this industry has being a huge success story in Ireland.

Course Options for the Study of Equestrian Science:

Many students pursue Equine Science at the two major University courses at UCD, and UL. Entry to Equine Science at UCD is through (DN250) Agriculture Science, while UL has offered its well-known BSc in Equine Science (LM093) for over thirty years. The UL course offers two streams; one which is geared towards Riding and Competing (Equitation) and the other more towards Business & Management roles within the industry. UL also offer a Level 6 option (LM180) to study Equine Science.

Zoology:

We are often asked to explain Zoology and there seems to be a good deal of confusion concerning the role of a Zoologist. While Animal Science in Ireland focuses largely on farm animals, Zoology as a Science looks at all animals. This can include the study of a wide variety of animals, from a reptile in a Zoo to a Pine Marten in an Irish Forest.

Jobs for Zoologists can be hard to find in Ireland. While a job as a keeper in a Zoo might be a dream job for a Zoology Graduate, openings in this sector are traditionally hard to find and Graduates are often frustrated by the lack of opportunities. Consequently, further studies at Post Graduate level are quite common, with many Graduates taking the academic route into research-based careers.

Studying Zoology has its own challenges as entry into courses is normally through General Entry Science at **UCD, UCC, NUIG** and **Trinity**. (See Section on Laboratory Sciences for more information) Points for these courses are traditionally high at around 500 plus, and in addition to this, students are expected to take Biology, Chemistry, Physics and Maths in Year One, before specialising in Zoology in Years Two, Three and Four

Wildlife Biology at **MTU** Tralee **(MT880)** is a lower point option at around 300 points. It is a particularly good course for those interested in studying Wildlife and Ecosystems within the island of Ireland.

Chapter Fourteen

Engineering

The Engineer/Designer:

Engineers impress us. They seem to have the ideal mix of skills and abilities and in most cases; they put them to good use. While academically strong, they also have excellent design skills, and like to be hands on with their work. Engineers are behind most of the improvements we see in everyday, modern life. They are leaders in innovation, who are currently fuelling the resurgence in manufacturing in Ireland today.

However, Engineers are not just involved in manufacturing, you will find that Engineers have played an important role in the development of most of the technological advances we see and use every day.

Are you naturally curious about how things work? Do you love solving problems? Do you enjoy making or designing things? Do you enjoy watching interesting documentaries about how things are made? Are you comfortable with Mathematics? If you answered **yes** to most of these questions, Engineering might be right for you! While everyone is different, most Engineers tend to exhibit these personality traits.

Engineering appeals to those students who have good academic ability but would also like to perform practical tasks or perhaps work a bit more in the outdoors.

Here is just a small flavour for what the various branches of Engineering cover.

Mechanical Engineers use their problem-solving skills to design machines and technologies that improve our world. They are primarily involved with optimising machines and/or engines of all types. From a high-speed conveyor system to a Formula 1 engine, they cover it all. Mechanical Engineering is very popular and is probably the most common of all the different Engineering specialities.

Civil, Structural and Environmental Engineers help to design and construct the buildings and infrastructure that are essential to modern society. Next time you are admiring that new bridge or indeed stadium, you can be sure that these Engineers played a major part in the design and overseeing of its safe construction. While there are many similarities between the various branches, the main emphasis of each could be very broadly summarised as; Structural Engineers are more involved at the initial design stage, Environmental Engineers help us understand the impact that any new building(s) may have on the environment. Finally, but importantly, Civil Engineers are responsible for overseeing construction projects and ensuring that the correct procedures are followed to guarantee that the building will be structurally sound and safe for human occupancy.

Electrical Engineers are heavily involved in the management of the Electricity Grid as well as overseeing the installation of a range of electrical projects, for example, floodlight systems at a stadium. As we make the transition from burning fossil fuels to using clean electricity, Electrical Engineers will play a very important role. As an example, Electrical Engineers will play a central role in designing and rolling out the infrastructure for electric vehicles.

Energy Engineers aim to increase energy efficiency and develop new technologies to reduce our dependence on fossil fuels. This discipline covers areas such as Wind Turbines, Solar Energy, Biofuels, and Wave/Tidal Power. It goes without saying that the need for qualified Energy Engineers is expected to be very strong over the coming years.

Electronic Engineers are at the heart of many of the technology devices we use every day. It's hard to think of many modern-day items that don't have some input from an electronic circuit. From your mobile phone to a microwave, it's the power of electronic technology that makes it all possible. Because of our reliance on electronics, this form of Engineering is predicted to be one of the top five demand careers in the world over the next twenty years.

Mechatronics combines Mechanical Engineering, Electronic Engineering and Software Engineering to design intelligent machines, such as robots and smart buildings.

Biomedical Engineers design and develop equipment and devices that help save people's lives. They design and improve a huge range of medical devices from a replacement knee joint to a pacemaker that can regulate a person's heart rate. It is a good combination of Engineering and Human Biology for a person interested in combining those subjects.

Biomedical Electronic combines the disciplines of Electronics and Biomedical Engineering for a fast developing career in the growing Medical Devices sector. For example the development of Continuous Glucose Monitors for those with Diabetes, eliminating the need for multiple finger pricking throughout the day to check levels.

Chemical and Process Engineers are involved in all kinds of industrial process developments, from the large-scale manufacture of pharmaceutical drugs to monitoring complex chemical reactions as for example in a petroleum refinery. A good ability and understanding of Chemistry is key to success in this role.

Aeronautical Engineers design and build aircraft, helicopters, satellites and other devices which travel through the air. They play a crucial role in improving safety for passengers on all modes of flying. Aeronautical Engineers play an important role in the maintenance of civilian and military aircraft.

Agricultural Engineers are involved in the design and improvement of all major types of agricultural machinery such as tractors, harvesters, and in some cases agricultural processing machinery and systems. This form of Engineering often appeals to students from farming backgrounds.

Marine Engineering involves the design, manufacture and maintenance of all types of ships, trawlers and sail boats. This discipline also covers equipment used at sea and on-board ships. Training to qualify as a Marine Engineer normally involves a period of training at sea.

Computer and Electronic Engineers are involved in developing the very latest technology devices. Being comfortable around computers helps as these Engineers are equally as comfortable with Software Development.

How to qualify as an Engineer:

Firstly, a word about Maths as it is probably the most important subject for all Engineering courses. Seven of our major Universities as well as some of our Technological Universities require Higher Level Maths at H4 grade as a minimum entry requirement into their Engineering Degrees. It is possible to study Engineering with Ordinary Level Maths at our five new Technological Universities. While these course options are mainly at Level 7 and 6 there are a number of Level 8 Degrees that accept Ordinary Level Maths.

We strongly recommend that any student considering Engineering should be comfortable with Maths (at least 03 as a general guideline). Other subjects that act as a good baseline for Engineering Degrees include Applied Maths, Physics, Engineering, Technology, D.C.G. and Chemistry.

Common Entry Engineering: These Degree courses allow students to take a general First Year (or Two Years at Trinity) before deciding which specialism they wish to pursue to Degree level. In addition, many of the top universities offer students two graduation options:

A. **Complete Four years and graduate at Honours Degree Level with a B.Eng.**

B. **Complete Five years study and graduate at Masters Level with an M.Eng.**

Engineers educated to **Masters Level** can apply directly to the Institute of Engineers in Ireland to become Chartered Engineers. Being a Chartered Engineering can lead to improved employment prospects in some cases, but it is not essential. There are alternative routes to becoming a Chartered Engineer.

Students should check the various college websites and check what options are available. We won't attempt to list all of the specialisms available through common entry engineering here, however to follow is a very brief summary of some options.

UCD (DN150): offers Mechanical Engineering and is the only college that offers Structural Engineering with Architecture. (Please note this course does not qualify the student as an Architect).

Trinity (TR032): offers a two-year window for students to decide what specialism to follow. Very good for those who are unsure about which area to specialize in.

DCU (DC200): well known for its options in Biomedical and Mechatronic Engineering.

TUD (TU805): has a strong track record for Structural and Building Services Engineering. **TUD** is well known for its practical approach to educating Engineers.

UCC (CK600): Chemical and Process Engineering option is very popular at **UCC.**

UL (LM116): offers options in Manufacturing and Design as well as Biomedical Engineering.

University of Galway (GY40): very broad offerings including Energy Systems Engineering. It is the **only** college that offers a specialism in Project & Construction Management.

Maynooth University (MH304): is best known for its Electronic Engineering Degree.

SETU Waterford **(SE700)**: has a good Common Entry Degree course that list Electrical/Electronic, Civil and Energy Engineering as specialisms to choose from.

MTU Cork (MT830): is highly regarded and has a strong reputation in Mechanical Engineering, and also offers a specialism in Structural Engineering.

Some Engineering disciplines **are not** available through Common Entry route and examples of these include:

Aeronautical & Aerospace Engineering include good options available at **UL (LM077)** and **SETU** Carlow **(SE714)**.

Agricultural Engineering **MTU** Tralee **(MT848)** having a strong reputation for this discipline with other options available at ATU Galway **(AU648)** and **SETU** Carlow, **(SE732 and SE733).**

Marine Engineering is only offered by **MTU** Cork **(MT764)** at the National **Maritime College** in Ringaskiddy.

ATU Athlone offers a variety of options to study Computer Engineering as well as a specific Degree in Polymer Engineering.

Dundalk IT offers a wide range of Engineering Degree options at around 350 points. **(DK843)**.

Studying Engineering at Level 6 & Level 7

All of the Technological Universities offer a wide range of options, most of which require qualifying grades in Ordinary Maths. Good progression opportunities exist for interested students to complete further studies up to Honours Degree Level.

We always recommend **TUD's** Level 7 Common Entry Engineering Degree **(TU709)** because of the breath of specialisms that it offers after First Year. Normal points for this course are around 400.

Most Technological Universities offer specialist courses and nearly all offer options in Mechanical, Electrical/Electronic or Civil Engineering. Points for these courses tend to average from 250 – 350 points.

There are also a number of **Engineering Based Apprenticeships** available. See section on Apprenticeships for more details.

Chapter Fifteen

Construction

Students who like the more practical Leaving Certificate Subjects of Construction Studies, Design Communication and Graphics (DCG), Engineering, Technology, and Art are often drawn to careers within the Construction sector. Those working in this area take pride in producing high standard quality work that results in tangible objects that can be viewed and enjoyed by many. If you feel you would enjoy working as part of a team of professionals in a practical way to design, develop and build outstanding structures then a career in the Construction sector might be for you.

We break down the Construction related careers into four roles: the Architect being the creative influence and Designer behind the building, the Architectural Technologist supporting the technical aspect of the planning process, maps and blueprints of the build, the Quantity Surveyor concerned with costings and regulations of the build and finally the Construction Manager taking overall responsibility and management of the entire cycle of the building project.

Architecture:

Every building and structure will normally have its origins with an Architect. An Architect is seen as the creative force behind the design of a building or structure. They have great spatial awareness and can envisage objects and shapes in 2D and 3D orientation. They are involved in the building process from initial concepts and planning right through to the finished project. They advise clients on the type, shape, and positioning of the building and the materials used internally and externally. In a nutshell Architects are concerned with the aesthetics and proper functionality of the buildings they design.

Architects have a good blend of technical skills and are knowledgeable in all areas of construction. They use computer aided software such as **AutoCAD** to produce detailed drawings. They may visit the building site to ensure that the construction of the building is in adherence to plans and design. They meet with clients to discuss possible amendments needed to the original design of the building.

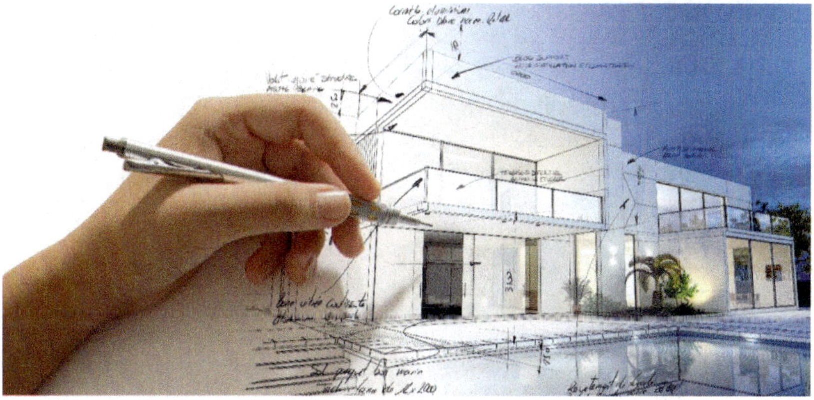

Architects need to take into account the environmental impact of the building and offer guidance and advice around sustainability. The Architect may guide the client through the process of seeking and gaining planning permission for the erection of the building or structure.

There are Six Undergraduate Degrees in Architecture available in Ireland. All courses are five years in duration. **Table 4.** shows a breakdown of the options available including entry requirements for each course. (While Art is not a requirement for any of the courses listed it is always recommended)

Table 4. Architecture Courses and Requirements

Main Features	**Content** ***Important Subjects***
TUD All applicants will be required to submit a **Portfolio** and attend an **Interview** as part of the admissions process. **Around Easter of Sixth Year Portfolio may contain Photographs, Imaginative Drawings, Paintings of Buildings and Places. Use of Pen, Pencil and other Media**	**CAO CODE: TU832** **HIGH POINTS 600+** Points awarded by combining **Leaving Certificate**, **Interview** and **Suitability Test Points** Students can gain up to **200 CAO** points based on the above **Suitability Test** and **Interview** **Points are not awarded** for the **Portfolio.**
UL **Portfolio not Required**	**CAO CODE: LM099** **POINTS LOW 500s**
UCD **Portfolio not Required**	**CAO CODE: DN100** **POINTS HIGH 500s**
UCC/MTU **Joint Programme** **Portfolio not Required**	**CAO CODE: CK606** **POINTS MID 500s**
SETU Waterford **Portfolio not Required**	**CAO CODE: SE701** **POINTS HIGH 300s**
ATU Sligo **Portfolio not Required**	**CAO CODE: AU925** **POINTS MID 400s**

Architectural Technologist:

Architectural Technologists will normally be found working in large Architectural firms, Manufacturing and Engineering Companies, as well as Planning Offices of a Local Authority. In general they are concerned with the technical aspects of the architectural design. They may be tasked with developing parts of designs that have to be scientifically accurate. They use design tools such as Building Information Modelling (BIM) or AutoCAD to draft and model their drawings.

The drawings that they develop are used to obtain planning permission and the Architectural Technologist is normally tasked with the administration of this process. The drawings are also used by the construction team on site to show them different angles of the build and to outline the positioning of electrics, broadband cables, sewerage and water. While they do need some creative skill there is much more focus on the need for technical skill and knowledge of the construction industry.

There are many options to study Architectural Technology. The courses are normally in the Technological Universities with popular choices in:

TUD Bolton Street Campus offers a Bachelor of Science (Honours) in Architectural Technology **(TU831)**.

SETU Carlow Campus offers a BSc in Architectural Technology **(SE702)**.

SETU Waterford Campus offers a BSc in Architectural & Building Information Modelling Technology **(SE703)**.

MTU offers a BSc in Architectural Technology **(MT859)**.

ATU Letterkenny, BSc in Architectural Technology **(AU343)**.

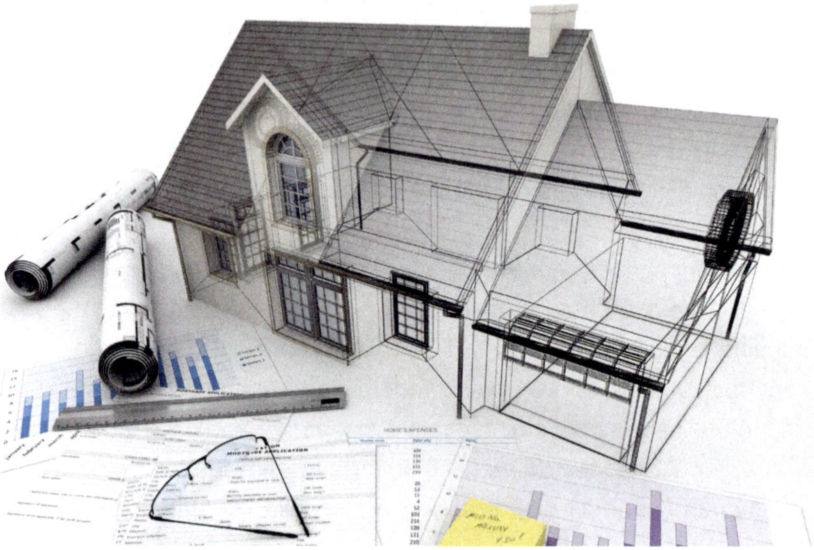

Quantity Surveyors:

The students who like Construction Studies but also like Business, Accounting or Economics Subjects often show an interest in Quantity Surveying. It is also the most popular of the construction related careers with the female cohort.

Quantity Surveyors are concerned with the cost of materials used within the construction industry, and the quality of these materials to ensure adherence with building and fire regulations. They focus on sourcing quality materials and guaranteeing that their client gets the best value for their money. Quantity Surveyors spend a lot of time negotiating prices with suppliers and ensuring that materials are available and delivered within the necessary timeline. They are tasked with sourcing materials locally and abroad and analysing what is the best value for money. They factor in all additional costs such as customs charges if appropriate, and also the delivery costs associated with getting the materials to site in a timely and cost efficient manner.

Sometimes Quantity Surveyors carry out site visits to take measurements and they use maps and blueprints to confirm these measurements are accurate before placing orders with their suppliers. Quantity Surveyors are involved in the tendering process for new building contracts and manage cost planning for the entire building project. As part of this they have to evaluate the risk of over spending and collaborate with Architects and Construction Managers to make sure this doesn't happen. It is the Quantity Surveyor's responsibility to negotiate claims for any extra costs or over spending that was not included in the original design or tender provided. You could say that the Quantity Surveyor is all about the money and the numbers involved in the entire cycle of a large or small building project.

Quantity Surveyors should have a methodical way of thinking, good financial and numerical skill in addition to excellent communication and negotiating skills.

Courses are available in the Technological Universities with the following being popular choices with students:

Bachelor of Science (Honours) in Quantity Surveying & Construction Economics (TU837) at TUD Bolton Street Campus. Points in the mid 400's

Lower point options averaging around 300 are available a number of other Technological Universities and Colleges including:

MTU Cork **(MT857)**, SETU Waterford **(SE704)**, TUS Athlone **(US880)**, Dundalk IT **(DK834)**, and ATU Letterkenny **(AU341)**.

Construction Management:

Construction Mangers are often referred to as Site Mangers. Regardless of the title they are responsible for all aspects and supervision of the building project. They must ensure that the project is completed on time and in a structured and sequenced format. They source, hire and supervise Construction Workers and Trades People to guarantee high standards of work.

A big concern for the Construction Manager is implementing health and safety on site and ensuring building standards are adhered to. For example, the Construction Manager must observe and confirm that the construction crew and all site visitors are wearing the proper protective personal equipment (PPE) such as hard hats, steel toe cap boots, and ear protectors. Failure to do so could result in a serious incident on site.

They also collaborate with Engineers, Quantity Surveyors and Architects to seek solutions to problems that arise on site. They work closely with Quantity Surveyors to monitor costs and to safeguard against any unnecessary costs or wastage on site. They monitor and review all stages of construction work to ensure compliance with building legislation and regulations.

Courses again are mostly available at the Technological Universities; however, both **UL** and **University of Galway also have good options:**

BSc in Construction Management and Engineering at **UL (LM082)**, points for this option tend to be in the mid 400's.

BSc Project and Construction Management at **University of Galway (GY410)**, points for this option tend to be high above 500.

BSc Construction Management at **TUD** Bolton Street, **(TU833)**, points 410+.

Lower point options that average around 300 points include:

TUS Limerick **(US885)**, **ATU** Galway **(AU635), SETU** Waterford BSc Construction Management & Engineering **(SE707)**, and **SETU** Carlow BSc Construction Management **(SE706)**.

Please note the above mentioned courses at **UL** and **SETU** with **Engineering** in the title **do not** qualify the individual in Engineering but gives the student a good grounding in Engineering principals related to the Construction sector.

Chapter Sixteen

Computer Science & Information Technology

Careers in the IT sector appeal to those with a genuine interest in Computer Science, and how these technologies are playing such an influential role in how modern society works. Without this core interest it is unlikely that students will embrace a Computer Science Degree and the learning involved.

Careers in Computer Science can be generally broken into two major sections: **Software and Hardware.**

Software and Software Development in particular focuses on Programming and Coding, while Hardware tends to focus on the technology that underpins Computer Networks and Systems, as well as the hardware associated with Desktops and Laptops etc.

It is not unusual for us to meet students in our practice that have already built their own computer from parts that they have purchased online. This is always a strong indicator that students are ready for a career in IT. A **good ability in Maths** is also essential to being successful in a Computer Science Degree. Leaving Certificate Physics is a useful subject to have studied also. Based on our experience in our practice, boys are much more likely to commit to Computer Science then girls.

For what seems like decades now careers in IT have been strong with almost full employment guaranteed for Software Developers and Hardware Engineers. Good Software Developers, or Programmers as they were previously known, are in constant demand and are primarily involved in writing software for a host of applications. Recent employment studies see strong demand continuing in the short to medium term.

Software Developers write code for a large variety of companies including Financial Services, App Development, and for large Social Media platforms. Web development is another key IT skill in huge demand all over the globe. Cyber-Security has become very important in recent times as companies scramble to protect our personal data in our online transactions. All of these sectors are expected to continue to grow over the coming years and positions will need to be filled by a constant flow of highly skilled Computer Science Graduates.

For those that specialise into **Computer Hardware**, roles in Management Information Systems (MIS) are popular with the advent of new regulations around data protection, it is now more important than ever to manage people's data securely.

Technical Support is another common role for the Hardware Engineer and often we find these people working for large Technical Support Companies. Within large organisations these tech support specialists are often best known for operating the **help desk** function.

Courses in Computer Science

All colleges provide a range of qualifications in the Computer Science areas. Most are four-years (BSc) Honours Degrees. There are a number of different sectors which you can train for and these include Programming (Software Development) writing software for a range of applications including mobile devices and apps. All colleges have solid options.

> **Trinity College** has probably been using and teaching computers longer than anyone. Their Degree **(TR033)** is among the most popular and it is currently **the only one** that requires Maths at H4 as an entry requirement.

As expected, the Dublin Universities command higher entry points levels with both **Trinity** and UCD **(DN201)** needing more than 540 points, while the popular **DCU** Course **(DC121)** is normally in the high 400's. UCC **(CK401)** and University of Galway **(GY350)** are competitively placed at around the low 500's when compared with some of the larger Dublin Universities.

Maynooth University offers students the chance to study Computer Science through their excellent BA Arts Degree **(MH101).** In this case students can select up to three other subjects in first year and this option suits those who may like computers but are unsure about making a full commitment to the discipline.

You can take a full Degree in Computer Science at any of the Technological Universities for around 300 points, with the exception of TUD **(TU856)** at between 450 and 500 points.

University of Limerick (UL) offers a number of courses, including Artificial Intelligence and Machine Learning **(LM174)** as well as Common Entry Computer Science **(LM121)**.

UL launched a new style learning model for Computer Sciences in the recent past. This course uses the American ***residency*** style of learning where up to 50% of the experience gained is from five structured paid work placements. It is possible to gain a full Master's Degree qualification from this course in four years. However, this course has entry requirements in the form of a Portfolio. (worth 300 points) in addition to standard Leaving Certificate points. Check the **UL** website for further details.

Games Development. It is possible to take a specialist Degree in Games Development. Graduates of these courses are involved in creating the latest games and technologies to support platforms like PlayStation and Xbox. Best course options include **SETU** Carlow **(SE607)**, UL via **(LM121)** and **TUD (TU984).**

Management of Information Systems (MIS). These courses focus on the management of data within large organisations. The resulting careers often include Technological Support and Network Technologies. **TUD's** Computer Science-Infrastructure **(TU857)** is an excellent option. **SETU** Waterford offer a route through their Common Entry Computer Science course called Cloud and Networks via **(SE600)**.

Another potential route into this area is through the study of Business Information Systems. For many years both **UCC (CK203)** and **MTU (MT944)** have been to the forefront delivering top class Degree courses in these combined disciplines. More recent additions include **ATU** Galway **(AU602)** and **SETU** Waterford **(SE413)**. For those who wish to study in Dublin, DCU offers a combination of Computer Science and Business in the same Degree **(DC120)**.

Multi Media. This discipline involves Computer Science with a little more emphasis on Creative Design, for example, Graphic Design. Sometimes used in the design and development of Web Sites and E-Learning materials. Well known courses include Creative Computing at the **Institute of Art Design and Technology**, Dun Laoghaire **(IADT) (DL836)** and SETU Waterford **(SE605)**.

Creative Media Technologies. Software Development geared towards industry sectors which have a high emphasis on Audio/Visual content. Well known courses include **IADT (DL838)** and Music Technology via Arts at **Maynooth (MH101)** which has a strong emphasis on Computerised Music Modules.

Cybercrime and Security. This increasingly important area focuses on Software Development which in turn is geared towards increasing the level of security to guard against fraud and Hackers. Strong course options are available at **TUD (TU863)**, **UL** via **(LM121)**, while **SETU** has options at both Waterford and Carlow Campuses **(SE602 and SE606)**.

Data Analytics. Another fast growing IT related area is Data Analytics, which focuses on analysing the vast amount of data we are currently generating. While attempting to see what this huge information resource is telling us as a society, it also aims to help companies gain a competitive advantage. Courses at **DCU**, Data Science **(DC123), ATU** Letterkenny **(AU363), Maynooth (MH207), National College of Ireland (NCI) (NC205)** and **UCC (CK411)**.

What does the future hold for careers in IT?

We are often asked this question particularly in relation to the advent of **Artificial Intelligence (AI).** The answer is we don't really know. To get some idea of what the future of an AI led world might look like, we asked **Chat GPT** itself what it thought.

How will the future for Software Development be affected by Artificial Intelligence. *The future of software development is poised to undergo significant transformations due to the rapid advancements in Artificial Intelligence (AI). Here are some of the key ways AI is expected to impact the field:*

1. Automation of Coding Tasks

Code Generation: *AI-driven tools like GitHub Copilot and OpenAI's Codex are already automating portions of code writing. These tools can suggest lines of code, entire functions, or even full projects based on a developer's input. This trend is likely to continue, with AI handling more routine coding tasks, allowing developers to focus on more complex and creative aspects of software development.*

Testing and Debugging: *AI can automatically generate test cases, identify bugs, and even suggest fixes. This can significantly speed up the software development lifecycle and reduce human error.*

2. Shift in Developer Roles

Higher-Level Focus: *As AI handles more of the mundane coding tasks, developers may increasingly focus on higher-level problem-solving, architecture design, and integrating AI solutions into their systems.*

New Skill Sets: *Developers will need to adapt by learning to work with AI tools, understand AI-driven code, and potentially develop skills in AI and machine learning (ML) themselves.*

3. Intelligent Software Design

AI-Driven Design Tools: *AI can help design software architecture, user interfaces, and even suggest optimal technology stacks. This could lead to more efficient and effective software solutions, reducing the time from concept to deployment.*

Adaptive and Learning Systems: *AI can create systems that learn and adapt to user behaviour over time, making software more intuitive and user centric. This could lead to the development of software that evolves based on how it's used.*

4. Increased Productivity and Collaboration

5. Impact on Software Quality and Security

Enhanced Security: *AI can identify security vulnerabilities in real-time, even in complex and large codebases. AI-driven tools can also automate the patching process, leading to more secure software.*

6. Democratization of Software Development

Citizen Developers: *With the help of AI, non-developers or citizen developers can create and manage their own software solutions, further blurring the lines between professional developers and end-users.*

7. Ethical and Governance Considerations

Ethical Coding Practices: *As AI takes on more development tasks, ensuring ethical use and the avoidance of bias in AI-generated code will be critical. Developers will need to be vigilant about the ethical implications of the AI tools they use.*

8. Job Market Dynamics

Demand for AI Expertise: *There will be a growing demand for developers who understand AI and ML, leading to a potential shift in the job market where AI-savvy developers are highly sought after.*

Potential Job Displacement: *While AI will create new roles, there is also a possibility of job displacement for those who are unable or unwilling to adapt to the new AI-driven landscape. This could lead to a need for reskilling and upskilling within the industry.*

9. New Opportunities for Innovation

AI-Powered Software Innovations: *The integration of AI into software development opens up new possibilities for creating innovative applications that were previously unimaginable.*

10. Changing the Nature of Software

The traditional paradigms of software development may evolve as AI becomes more integrated, leading to new methodologies, frameworks, and best practices.

Conclusion

The future of Software Development in the age of AI will be marked by increased automation, a shift in developer roles, and the emergence of new tools and methodologies. While this presents significant opportunities for innovation and efficiency, it also brings challenges in terms of ethics, job displacement, and the need for continuous learning and adaptation. Developers who can harness the power of AI while navigating these challenges will be well-positioned for success in this evolving landscape.

Chapter Seventeen

Apprenticeships

In some respects there has been significant change in the Apprenticeship sector in Ireland. Traditionally when people think of Apprenticeships they think of Carpentry, Electricians or perhaps a Motor Mechanic. Nowadays, Apprenticeships cover a much broader array of careers. These new Apprenticeships cover Financial Services areas such as Accounting Technician or Property Management, while another growing sector for Apprentices is the Insurance sector. Here successful students can work and gain experience in the Insurance sector while studying for a full Level 8 Honours Degree.

Apprenticeships have also been developed for a range of careers across the Hospitality and Culinary Arts / Cheffing sectors. To see a full list of the over seventy Apprenticeships that are available please visit **www.apprentices.ie** .

Entry routes and training can be different for the various Apprenticeships. For the purpose of this chapter, we will break Apprenticeships down into two broad categories:

1. Traditional Craft Based Apprenticeships

2. Non-traditional Apprenticeships such as Specialist Apprentice ships in the Financial Sector.

Craft Based Apprenticeships:

In Ireland today all Apprenticeships are managed by Solas. Solas as an organisation is part of the Education and Training Board (ETB) structure nationwide which has largely replaced its predecessor FAS. Craft based Apprenticeships haven't changed much over the years and the training is referred to as Standard Based Apprenticeship Training. This route takes four years to complete and roughly breaks down into one year spent in college and the other three years spent on the job with an employer.

The best-known craft Apprenticeships are Carpentry, Plumbing, Block-laying and the ever popular Electrician. These Apprenticeships are mainly linked to the Construction sector. Young people can also enter into Engineering Apprenticeships, with the most popular of these being Mechanic, including Motor, Agricultural and Heavy Vehicle, Fabrication and Welding, Precision Engineering (CNC Lathe) Maintenance

Fitter, and Auto Body repair. There are of course many other less well-known Apprenticeships. See the full list on www.apprentices.ie for more details.

Apprenticeships as a career in our opinion does not get enough attention within the school guidance system. Many of our clients seem genuinely confused about how to successfully secure an Apprenticeship.

For those young people that are interested we advise the following:

First and foremost when considering an Apprenticeship young people should be thinking about getting a **JOB**. After all, the first step in any Apprenticeship is going to work.

Like applying for any job it is very important to have a good **CV**. This can be challenging sometimes for young people of a school going age, and they may need help in preparing one.

A good tip for any young person doing up a CV is to make sure that they emphasise all practical experiences, for example, Practical Subjects studied in school, projects completed, and in particular detail, any relevant work experience completed.

It is one thing having a good CV; it is another step getting it out to potential employers. Applicants can have a different approach to this, and we recommend some or all of the following.

Make a list of employers for example garages/main dealerships (or whatever is relevant to the sector) and get a copy of the CV into all of them.

Circulate the CV at the local sports club. Sports Club car parks can be great location to spot local contractors vans!

Make sure that parents have a copy to hand when the meet work colleagues or when trades people arrive to do work in the house.
Call in family favours and get all family members to circulate the CV among their contacts.

The above steps can be seen as a good measure of how badly the student wants the Apprenticeship.

What they put into this process will come back.

One thing we are pretty sure about is that very few young people have employers calling to their family home asking them if they would like to sign up to their Company.

Non-Traditional Apprenticeships:

The Apprenticeship sector has grown considerably over the past five to ten years. New Apprenticeships are being developed all the time and currently there are around seventy Apprenticeships available in Ireland. Sectors which have experienced the most growth include Financial, Hospitality, Agriculture, Logistics and IT. These new Apprenticeships incorporate an ***'earn as you learn'*** approach, and many include a recognised third level qualification. These qualifications can range from a level 6 Higher Certificate to a level 9 Master's Degree, as for example the new Apprenticeship in Quantity Surveying or Social Work.

Many of the Financial Apprenticeships are structured similarly and students work four days per week with their host company while spending one day per week in college studying for their qualification.

Most Apprenticeships in the Financial sector earn salaries in the mid €20,000 bracket. Some Apprenticeships such as the popular Insurance Practitioner allow the participant to study for a full level 8 Honours Degree. Other popular Financial Apprenticeships include Real Estate and Accounting Technician.

How to become an Apprentice in these sectors:

Most of these Apprenticeships have a sponsoring organization or company. In the case of Accounting Technicians' applications are managed by **Accounting Technicians Ireland (ATI).**

For those interested in completing an Insurance Apprenticeship, you normally apply to the sponsoring Company, for example Zurich or Campion Insurance.

More information can be found on the Apprenticeship website; **www.apprentices.ie** .

Chapter Eighteen

Post Leaving Certificate Courses (PLC) and Tertiary Degrees

Colleges of Further Education are the normal providers of PLC Courses. Applications are made directly to these colleges, and there is no need to apply through the CAO. There are a large range of courses to choose from including childcare, sports, art, business, science, engineering, beauty therapy, hairdressing nursing studies, and pre university studies.

There are a number of reasons why a student would consider completing a PLC Course.

Some PLC Courses can lead directly into employment. Popular options here include Childcare, Leisure Studies (for working in Gyms/ Leisure Centres) and Agriculture at the Teagasc Colleges around the country.

On completion of a 1 year PLC course, successful students are awarded a QQI Level 5 Qualification and in the examples above, this is the minimum requirement for entry into employment in these careers.

Some courses have an option which allows students to continue their studies for another year. The qualification conferred is then a QQI Level 6 Award. These are often 'Special Purpose' awards or in the case of Beauty Therapy and Hairdressing the QQI Level 6 is the normal requirement for full qualification.

Another reason for students to consider a PLC course is to equip them with the knowledge they need to increase their chances of success in a third level course of interest. For example, where a student is keen to study engineering but may not have had the opportunity to study technological subjects at Leaving Certificate level, then we often suggest that they take a PLC course called Pre University Engineering, where this knowledge gap will be addressed. We sometimes refer to this as 'Bridging Studies'.

Another popular Pre-University course is an Art Portfolio course. In this situation a student may need an Art Portfolio as part of the Entry Requirements for a design related course. In some cases it may not be possible to complete this portfolio during the Leaving Certificate year. So, a student may take a gap year to complete their Art Portfolio for example at 'Gorey School of Art'.

Students can also use their QQI Award(s) to help them improve their access to a range of degree courses in the UK and Europe.

PLC Course Points System

Students can use the points accumulated from their QQI Level 5/6 PLC course to apply via the CAO for entry into a range of Third Level linked courses. Let's break down how the QQI points system works;

Students must complete 8 Modules to achieve a full QQI award. Each course has a Communications and Work Experience Module included.

The marking system for the QQI Award is broken down as

Distinction:	(80%+),
Merit:	(65%-79%),
Pass:	(50%-64%),
Unsuccessful:	(0%- 49%).

Points are awarded for each module as follows;

Distinction = 50pts Merit = 35pts Pass = 20pts.

So for example: 3 Distinctions + 5 Merits = 325pts.

(50x3) = 150 + (35 x 5) = 175 = Total of 325 pts

In a situation where the points gained from the PLC course exceeds the points scored at Leaving Certificate, then the improved PLC Points can be used to access 3rd Level College Courses.

Please Note: Students who have completed **Leaving Certificate Applied** must use the PLC route and Points system outlined above if they wish to access Third Level College.

Some Colleges of Further Education have links in to certain Third Level Colleges.

In certain cases students must complete a specific PLC that is directly linked to the Third Level Course they wish to pursue. Colleges reserve a small amount of places for students that have successfully completed linked PLC courses. Securing one of these places is a competitive process and there are no guarantees of being successful in securing a place.

For those wishing to enter a Level 8 Honours Degree using their QQI Award they must present with a minimum of 3 Distinctions. In some cases, 5 distinctions are needed. In general students need to achieve very good results to give themselves a realistic chance of being successful in landing one of the reserved places.

Applicant should research this route thoroughly by using the search option on the CAO website and also check the links on the Third Level Course Information page.

Technological Universities have more places available for students accessing courses with their QQI award then the traditional universities. A full QQI Level 5 award is accepted as meeting the minimum entry requirements for courses at the Technological Universities provided that the QQI points total equals the amount of points required by the CAO for that particular course.

(Please note some courses have specific LC subject requirements in addition to your QQI Award).

The structure of PLC courses can differ from course to course. Some students will spend 4 days a week in college and 1 day on work experience, while for others their work experience is completed over a block period of 2 weeks.

How to apply for a PLC?

The first step is for a student to research courses available by using the Qualifax course search facility. Once the student has reviewed the entry requirements and structure of their chosen course and the direct Third Level links available from this course they can use the **'Apply'** button on the course information page. Here the student will set up an account on the Fetch Course Platform and make a simple application for their desired course via this platform.

The next step is usually an interview. If successful at interview and if all minimum Leaving Certificate requirements are achieved the student may receive confirmation of their place.

Students can apply for the PLC's courses anytime from January of 6th year right through to September. It is advised to apply as early as possible.

Tertiary Degrees:

The Tertiary Degree programme is a recent initiative and was launched in 2023. This education pathway is co facilitated and managed by the localised ETBs in conjunction with certain Higher Education providers. The goal of The Tertiary Degrees is to provide an easier route for students to access Third Level education outside of the competitive CAO point's race. To facilitate this option the two managing bodies have come together and developed specific further education pathways which allow direct progression from specific PLC Courses to the linked course in the Third Level provider. The good news is that students do not have to worry about having the required CAO points in order to access these courses!

How do the tertiary degrees work?

There are a vast number of degree options available through the Tertiary pathway with new options being added all the time. There are currently options available in Music, Media Production, Science, IT, Engineering, Business, General and Mental Health Nursing, Occupational Therapy and Social Work. The structure of the degree is broken down between time spent studying in one of the many Colleges of Further Education and time spent studying in the Third Level College. The majority of the courses involve the student spending 1 year in a College of Further Education and 3 Years in the Third Level College.

However, there are some exceptions here notably for the Nursing and Occupational Therapy options. In this situation students will spend 1 year in the College of Further Education and a full 4 years in the partnered Third Level College. Another notable exception is Audio Music Production where the degree is broken down into 2 years in the College of Further Education and 2 years in the Third Level College.

After completion of the Further Education element the student will be awarded a QQI Award, and after completion of the Third Level element the student will be awarded their Level 7 or Level 8 Hons Degree depending on what option they applied for.

While progression to the Third Level College element is streamlined, students must pass their QQI exams. Once again a notable exception here is the Nursing option where students who wish to progress must achieve a specific standard in their QQI award. This standard is currently set at the student achieving, a minimum five distinctions, which must include Anatomy and Physiology, Introduction to Nursing Theory and Practice and Human Growth and Development or Biology.

How to apply for a Tertiary Degree?

The first step is for applicants to check out the array of courses available. They can do this on the National Tertiary Office (NTO) website ***https://nto.hea.ie/courses/*** . Once the student has reviewed the entry requirements and structure of their chosen course, they can use the **'Apply'** button on the course information page. This button will direct the student to Fetch Courses ***https://www.fetchcourses.ie/***. Here the student will set up an account and make a simple application for their desired course via this platform.

The next step is usually an interview. If successful at interview and if all minimum Leaving Certificate requirements are achieved, the student may receive confirmation of their place. **Please note** there are a set of minimum requirements attached to all courses and students are urged to research this prior to applying.

Students can apply for the Tertiary Degrees from February up to late September depending on availability.

Students often ask us should they apply for the Tertiary Degree or the Linked PLC pathway.

There is no right or wrong answer here as it is based on the student's individual situation and their reason for considering these options. However, one of the main advantages of the Tertiary Degree is that you are guaranteed your route into Third Level Education (subject to passing QQI exams) whereas the Linked PLC pathway puts you back into the competitive CAO points race to access college with no guarantee of success.

Chapter Nineteen

Overview of the CAO System in Ireland

The Central Applications Office (CAO) is the organization responsible for managing applications to undergraduate courses in higher education institutions in Ireland. Established to streamline the application process, the CAO serves as a centralized platform where students can apply to multiple colleges and universities across the country using a single application form.

How does the CAO System Work?

Application Process:

- **Registration:** Prospective students begin by creating an account on the CAO website by using the '**Apply**' button on the CAO home page. This involves providing personal details, such as name, date of birth, and contact information and paying the application fee. Once these steps are completed students will receive their **CAO Number**. This number must be recorded and kept safe as it will be needed to re-enter your CAO account in the future and for all correspondence with the CAO.

- **Course Selection:** Students can apply for up to ten courses in two lists—**Level 8** (Honours Degree) and **Level 6/7** (Ordinary Degree/Higher Certificate). Courses are listed in order of preference, with the most desired course listed first. It's important that applicants choose their course preferences carefully, as the order in which they list them determines the sequence in which they will be considered during the Offers Process.

- **Application Deadline:** The CAO has several key deadlines throughout the year. The most important are the **1st February** for the normal closing date and **1st July** for the change-of-mind facility, which allows students to adjust their course preferences.

Offer Process:

- **Leaving Certificate Results:** Offers are made based on the results of the Leaving Certificate. Each course has a minimum entry requirement and a points threshold, calculated using the CAO Points Scale. **Points are awarded based on the student's performance in their six best subjects.**

- **Round Offers:** After the Leaving Certificate results are released, the CAO issues offers in several rounds, typically starting in mid-August. In each round, students may receive an offer for the highest-preference course for which they meet the requirements and points threshold.

- **Acceptance of Offers:** Once an offer is made, the student can either accept or decline it. If accepted, the student is removed from consideration for lower-preference courses submitted on their CAO but remains eligible for higher-preference courses submitted on their CAO in subsequent rounds if their points meet the requirements.

Special Categories:

- **Restricted Courses:** Some courses, such as those in art, music, or medicine, require additional assessments like portfolios, interviews, or aptitude tests. These courses must be listed by **1st February** and cannot be changed later using the change-of-mind facility.

- **HEAR and DARE Schemes:** The CAO also accommodates students applying through the **Higher Education Access Route (HEAR)** and **Disability Access Route to Education (DARE)**, which provide additional support and consideration for students from disadvantaged backgrounds or with disabilities.

Important Considerations:

- **Order of Preference:** Students must be strategic in listing their course preferences. If a student receives an offer and accepts it, they cannot subsequently receive an offer for a lower-preference course on their CAO, even if they meet the requirements.

- **Deferred Entry:** Students who wish to defer their place for a year can apply to the institution for a deferral once an offer is made. If granted, they must reapply the following year to take up the place. Please note it is at the Institutions discretion if they deferral is granted or not.

Change of Mind:

- **Flexibility:** The CAO provides a **Change of Mind** facility from **May 5th to July 1st** each year. During this period, students can change their course preferences without additional cost. This allows students to reassess their choices based on new information or personal circumstances. The student will use the **'My Application'** on the CAO home page to re-enter their CAO.

The CAO system ensures a transparent process for students applying to higher education institutions in Ireland. By managing applications centrally, the CAO simplifies the process for students, allowing them to apply to multiple courses and institutions efficiently.

HEAR & DARE Schemes:

The HEAR (Higher Education Access Route) and DARE (Disability Access Route to Education) schemes are special access routes for students applying to higher education in Ireland through the CAO. They are designed to provide additional support and opportunities for students who face particular challenges in accessing higher education.

HEAR Scheme (Higher Education Access Route)

Purpose:

The HEAR scheme is aimed at supporting students from socio-economically disadvantaged backgrounds. It provides eligible students with reduced points offers and extra college supports, such as academic, personal, and financial assistance, to help them succeed in higher education.

Eligibility Criteria:

To qualify for HEAR, students must meet a combination of socio-economic indicators, including:

1. **Income:** The household income must be below a certain threshold, which varies depending on family size.
2. **Medical Card:** The family must hold a Medical Card or GP Visit Card.
3. **Means-Tested Social Welfare:** The family must be in receipt of means-tested social welfare payments.
4. DEIS School Attendance: The student must have attended a DEIS school for at least five years.
5. **Socio-Economic Group:** The student's parents or guardians must belong to a socio-economic group that is underrepresented in higher education

6. **Living in a Disadvantaged Area:** The student must live in an area of concentrated disadvantage, as determined by the Irish government's Pobal HP Deprivation Index.

Application Process:

- **CAO Application:** Students apply to HEAR through the CAO by indicating their interest and completing the HEAR section of the online CAO application form.
- **Supporting Documents:** Applicants must submit various documents to verify their eligibility, such as proof of income, medical card details, and social welfare statements.
- **Application Deadline:** The HEAR application must be completed by the **1st February,** and supporting documents must be submitted by the **15th March.**

Benefits:

- **Reduced Points Offers:** HEAR students may receive offers at reduced points for their chosen courses, though they must still meet the minimum entry requirements.
- **Additional Support:** Once enrolled, HEAR students receive various forms of support, including orientation programs, academic tutoring, financial aid, and personal development workshops.

DARE Scheme (Disability Access Route to Education)

Purpose:

The DARE scheme is designed to support students with disabilities in accessing higher education. It offers reduced points places and tailored supports to students whose disabilities have impacted their educational performance.

Eligibility Criteria:

To qualify for DARE, students must meet the following:

- **Disability Category:** Students must have a disability that falls into one of the categories recognized by DARE, such as a physical disability, sensory impairment, specific learning difficulty (like dyslexia), mental health condition, or other significant ongoing illness.
- **Impact Statement:** The student must provide a detailed impact statement outlining how their disability has affected their learning and academic performance.
- **Evidence of Disability:** Applicants must submit an evidence of disability form completed by a medical professional, confirming the nature and extent of the disability.

Application Process:

- **CAO Application:** Like HEAR, students apply to DARE through the CAO by completing the DARE section of the application form.
- **Supporting Documents:** Students must provide supporting documentation, including the impact statement and evidence of disability, by 15th March.
- **Educational Impact Statement:** This is usually filled out by the student's school to demonstrate how the disability has affected their secondary education.

Benefits:

- **Reduced Points Offers:** Eligible DARE students may receive course offers at reduced points if their disability has significantly impacted their education, as long as they meet the basic course requirements.

- **Additional Supports:** Once in college, DARE students can access various supports, including assistive technology, learning support services, exam accommodations, and orientation programs tailored to their needs.

HEAR and DARE Common Features

- **Supporting Documents**: Both schemes require the submission of extensive supporting documentation to confirm eligibility. Failure to submit the required documents by the deadline will disqualify the application.
- **Dual Eligibility:** Some students may be eligible for both HEAR and DARE, in which case they can apply for both. This could provide a greater level of support and more opportunities for reduced points offers.
- **Pre-College Preparation:** Successful applicants in both schemes may have the opportunity to participate in pre-college preparation programs, which help ease the transition to higher education by familiarizing students with campus life, study skills, and available supports.

A Reminder of the Important Deadlines

- **1st February:** Deadline to apply for HEAR and DARE on the CAO application.
- **15th March:** Deadline to submit supporting documents.

Both the HEAR and DARE schemes are essential in ensuring that higher education in Ireland is accessible to all students, regardless of their socio-economic background or disabilities. These schemes aim to level the playing field, giving eligible students the chance to succeed in their academic and professional lives.

Chapter Twenty

Studying in the United Kingdom, Northern Ireland and Europe.

<u>**United Kingdom and Northern Ireland:**</u>

Any student who wishes to study a full-time undergraduate degree in the UK or NI will submit their application via the centralised application platform University and Colleges Admissions Service' referred to as UCAS. UCAS will in turn send all applications to the relevant colleges where the assessment process begins.

Entry into courses in the UK and NI is not based solely on the points system as per the CAO. It is based on a number of factors including, personal statement, academic reference, interview and /or test and in most cases subject specific minimum leaving certificate grades. Some colleges however, will refer to a tariff point requirement. Please see **Table 5** for the tariff points comparison to Irish Leaving Certificate Grades. The tariff points can be calculated based on 5 but normally 6 subjects depending on the specific college / course.

There are a number of stages and deadlines involved in making a UCAS application. Here is a breakdown of what is involved.

Students will set up a UCAS account on ***www.ucas.com***. This account will be where all communications are managed between the student and the colleges applied to. Students normally set up this account the year prior to intake into college. However students can not submit their application until early September of 6th Year.

The deadline for submitting an application for the majority of courses is normally the last week of January. However, the deadline for submitting an UCAS application for all courses in Oxford and Cambridge and all courses in Medicine, Dentistry, and Veterinary Medicine is October 15th.

For Art and Design related courses the deadline is extended to the last week of March. We strongly encourage students to check all deadlines to avoid disappointment.

Students should use the UCAS platform to research all courses of interest. There is a wealth of information on this website including course description, application process, course entry requirements, college fees and contact details for all the individual colleges.

Students can apply for up to 5 courses on their UCAS application. This can be 5 courses in one college or a range of courses in different colleges. Course choices should be submitted in alphabetical order. Please note order of preference is not applicable here. If applying for medicine you can only include 4 options to study medicine on your application.

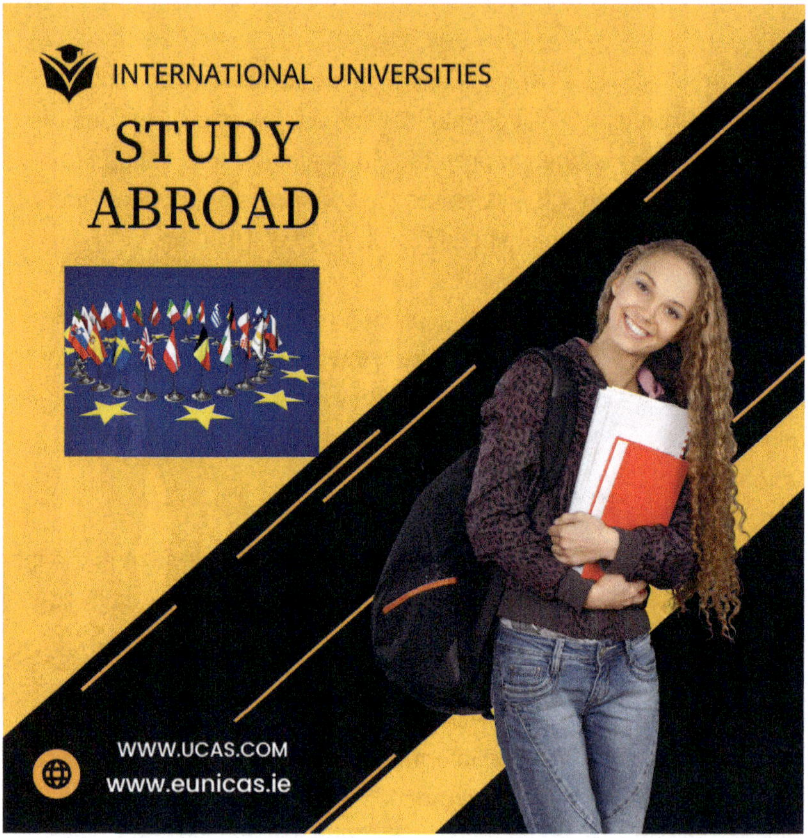

Now into the 'nitty gritty' of the application. All UCAS applicants must write a personal statement. The personal statement is approximately 4,000 characters (not words) in length. The personal statement gives you the chance to shine and to tell the colleges about yourself, your academic expectations, why you want to study in the UK, your interest in the chosen area, and to detail any extracurricular activities that might be relevant to the area you wish to study.

The personal statement is a big part of the application process and should be taken seriously. It needs to be of a high standard. It is advised to write at least **3 drafts** before finalising it and always get a competent person to review it on your behalf. Many schools will assist students with this. We advise students to work on this personal statement between the summers of 5th and 6th year to avoid rushing it to reach relevant deadlines.

You must also provide a letter of recommendation or reference to UCAS, which is usually provided by your school. Ask your Principal or Career Guidance Teacher for this early in the school year. Once all this information is collated by UCAS it is sent to the relevant colleges.

The colleges will review all completed applications. At this stage applicants may be called for interview and / or some form of additional test / audition depending on what is being applied for. **The majority of applicants will have to do an interview.** The interviews can run anytime form February right through to Easter and may be in person or online. Students will receive notification of this interview via their account and by email. The interviews / tests / auditions help the colleges to compare applicants before making the offers.

Students can use 'The Track' Facility in their account to see how their application is progressing: Has it gone to the colleges? Has the college reviewed it? Am I being called for an interview? Students will also use this facility to check if they have received any college offers.

The offers from the UK / NI colleges are normally available by the middle of May. Students must accept offers by early June approximately June 9th. There are two types of offers that an applicant can receive:

When an applicant gets an **'unconditional offer'** this means that they have met all academic requirements needed for the course and the place is theirs if they wish to avail of it.

A **'conditional offer'** means that they need to meet all academic requirements (i.e. Leaving Certificate Grades / Tariff Points) to be guaranteed this place.

Students will use 'The Track' Facility to accept their offers. There are 2 types of acceptance that you can make to an offer.

If you get an offer of your chosen course you accept this as your **'Firm Acceptance'**.

If you get another offer you accept this as your **'Insurance Acceptance'** in case you don't achieve the academic requirements for your 'firm acceptance' of your conditional offer.

Students can also use the **'Clearing Section'** on the UCAS website to make a late application to the UK / NI colleges. Students who have previously applied through UCAS in the same year can use 'Clearing' for any course they did not receive an offer for or have previously applied to. Students who did not make a UCAS application can also use 'Clearing'.

Students can even use this option on the day they get their Leaving Certificate results or College offers in Ireland. Students who make these late applications via 'Clearing' will follow the procedures set out under the information on the specific course page. We advise students who are using 'Clearing' at this late stage to contact the individual college directly for instructions.

If you are considering a late 'Clearing' application do bear in mind if successful you will be heading to the UK to commence your studies within a quick timeframe of 1 to 2 weeks from the date of receiving your offer. It is a good idea to keep an eye on 'Clearing' as we have seen students year on year getting offers via 'Clearing' for high demand areas such as pharmacy, nursing, occupational therapy and speech and language therapy to mention just a few.

The financial side of studying in the UK and NI:

All Irish students who are studying in the UK are currently considered 'home students' which basically translates to them being able to avail of the same college fees as UK citizens. The College fees are approximately £9,500 (sterling) per year.

Students opting to study in NI have considerable cheaper fees coming in at approximately £4,000 (sterling) per year.

Students must also take into account accommodation costs, living expenses and travelling back and forward between Ireland and UK when necessary.

So, in summary the main point we always impart to students considering studying in the UK is to **start the process early**. Engage in research, speak to students who have done it before, visit the colleges you are considering if possible and as a family sit down discuss all the pros and cons of a potential move to the UK.

Table 5. Detailing Tariff points comparison to Irish Leaving Certificate Grades.

Irish Leaving Certificate Grade ⟷	Tariff Point
H1	36
H2	30
H3	24
H4	18
H5	12
H6	9
O1	12
O2	10
O3	8
O4	6

Studying in Europe:

Studying in Europe has grown in popularity over recent years. For many years it was only students who wished to study the high demand courses in Ireland such veterinary, medicine, dentistry, physiotherapy and pharmacy who showed an interest in studying abroad particularly in Poland and Hungary. More recently students are choosing to explore other options in Europe including the areas of business, international relations, engineering, computer science and social sciences. In fact, many students coming to us for support voice the need to spread their wings outside of Ireland and to gain more of an international perspective during their college experience.

> In many cases but not all the attraction lies in the lower fees, the financial assistance available such as the grants and low interest loans from the chosen EU country. In addition, Irish students if eligible can be supported by the SUSI grant while studying in Europe.

Further to this, students don't have to battle for a college place based on the competitive Points Race as they do under the Irish CAO system. Students wishing to study in Europe will generally be assessed on achieving the minimum entry requirements: five passes in the Leaving Certificate Exam, plus one of or a combination of the following: a letter of motivation or personal statement, interview, entrance exam or multiple-choice test. Largely, it is easier and cheaper to get accommodation in these European Countries than here in Ireland. However, there are some reports that students are now starting to find it more difficult to source good standard and safe accommodation abroad.

For many considering studying in Europe their primary research starts with the valuable platform 'European Universities Central Application Support Service' more commonly known as EUNICAS. While EUNICAS is not an applications portal to the European Universities, it gives students independent information and support throughout the application process. We always advise students who are considering studying in Europe to register with EUNICAS - there is a small fee attached but it is well worth the investment. By doing this the student will have access to support on choosing the correct course, a step by step guide on applying, advice on the full application process including; any tests, interviews or personal statements that may be part of the

the process. They also offer information on finance and sourcing accommodation and as such EUNICAS is a very comprehensive and informative platform for students to avail of.

When applying to colleges in Europe areas for research include:

Further to using EUNICAS students and parents need to engage in additional research.

One of the main areas we encourage students to establish is 'whether or not the course is taught through English'. This seems like common sense, but more common is that students turn up to our sessions with a list of European Courses of interest that are NOT taught via English. Deadlines - applicants should check deadlines for applications as this differs greatly across all European Countries.

It is important to check out Visa requirements and Residency Requirements well in advance of any application being made. Residency requirements may impact the funding and grants available to Irish students, and this is particularly relevant for those considering studying in Sweden.

Some countries will require applicants to have their Leaving Certificate Qualifications verified or accredited so do check this out specifically if you are considering Spain.

Private vs Public Colleges - this can have a big impact on the fees that you pay.

Is there additional funding available from the country of interest and what is the qualifying criteria involved?

Is there campus accommodation and how do you apply for this? If not where is accommodation available, what are the fees, is it in a safe and convenient location?

Will you need transcripts from your Post Primary School and do they need to be transcribed to the language of your chosen country?

Finally, we encourage students to research how to submit their application as there is no Centralised European Platform or indeed for many Countries there is no single Centralised Application Platform such as the CAO or the UK's UCAS Platform.

For example, for those wishing to apply to Polish, Hungarian, Slovakian, Spanish and Italian Universities they make the application directly to the college using the college specific website portal.

The **Netherlands** remains one of the most popular choices with Irish Students. For those wishing to apply to the Netherlands they will use the Centralised Platform (Studielink.nl) to make their application. With many courses taught through English, the University of Groningen continues to be the most popular choice for Irish Students wishing to study in the Netherlands. Watch out for seminars in Ireland which are hosted by several Dutch Universities. These are an excellent source of information about specific colleges and the courses they offer.

There is also a Centralised Application process in Sweden, and this platform can be found at universityadmissions.se. All applications will be made online via this platform.

Finland operates a central applications platform Studyinfo.fi but applicants can also apply directly to the college via their website portal. Where you make your application depends on what and where you wish to study.

With a vast quantity of courses and many universities available to Irish Students in Europe it is very difficult to condense them all into this script. As such we encourage all interested parties to check out EUNICAS to support them through this process.

Some things to consider before making your application:

We always encourage students and parents to take a flight and visit the country and universities of interest before committing.
Research the frequency and cost of flights back and forward. Check out the distance from airport to university / accommodation (train or bus options).

Make sure your passport is in date.
Check out what is involved in setting up a bank account in your chosen country? Do you need to do this? OR will your Irish bank account suffice?

Research what medical care is like in your chosen country.
Note: Students can apply for a European Health Insurance Card (EHIC), through their local health centre in Ireland. This will cover them for a certain standard of health care if studying abroad for the academic year.

Students need to reflect on how they will cope with the rigours of living and studying in another country. Get up to speed with the local laws and etiquette of this country and always remember to act accordingly.

Students need to reflect on how they will feel entering a brand-new culture, language and different food choices.

There are challenges attached to studying abroad and homesickness and missing friends can be difficult at times. However, feedback from those that have gone on to graduate from European Universities is positive and they feel it is well worth any initial challenges they faced in the early days of their time abroad.

Abbreviations

ATU	Atlantic Technological University
B.Dent. Sc	Bachelor of Dental Science
B.Soc.Sc	Bachelor of Social Science
BA	Bachelor of Arts
BBS	Bachelor of Business Studies
BCL	Bachelor of Civil Law
BComm	Bachelor of Commerce
BEd	Bachelor of Education
BSc	Bachelor of Science
BSW	Bachelor of Social Work
CAO	Central Applications Office
DCG	Design Communication and Graphics
DCU	Dublin City University
ETB	Education and Training Boards
EUNICAS	European Universities Central Application Support Service.

GAMSATs	Graduate Medical School Admissions Test
HPATs	Health Professions Admission Test
IATD	Institute of Art, Design and Technology
LLB	Bachelor of Law
LSAD	Limerick School of Art and Design
MPharm	Masters in Pharmacy
MSc	Masters of Science
MTU	Munster Technological University
NCAD	National College of Art and Design
PE	Physical Education
PGCE	Post Graduate Certificate in Education
PGDE	Post Graduate Diploma in Education
PHD	Doctor of Philosophy
PLC	Post Leaving Certificate
PME	Professional Masters of Education
QQI	Quality Qualifications Ireland
RCSI	Royal College of Surgeons Ireland
SETU	South East Technological University
STEM	Science, Technology, Engineering, Maths.

SUSI	Student Universal Support Ireland
TUD	Technological University Dublin
TUS	Technological University of the Shannon
UCAS	Universities and Colleges Admissions Service
UCC	University College Cork
UCD	University College Dublin
UL	University of Limerick

Acknowledgments

It is always difficult when writing acknowledgements as to who to include and to ensure you include all relevant people. Here is our best attempt and we apologise to anyone left out.

Firstly, we have to acknowledge all the wonderful clients we have worked with throughout our many years of practice. Thank you all for choosing us and putting your trust in us and supporting us. Without you there would be no us and no book. We have met some wholesome people in our work and have kept in contact with many outside of the role of career guidance. Thank You.

Thank you to our families and friends those gone before us and those still with us. Without our families believe in us, unending support and understanding we could not do this work. A significant word of thanks and gratitude to Seamus' wife Lori and Mary's husband Sean.

To the many colleagues we have worked with in Whitney Career Guidance over the years, thank you all. We are blessed to call you friends. Thank you to Brid Colloton and Emma Donohue who worked with us in Whitney Career Guidance. Their ability to keep us and the office organised and their good cheer always added to an enjoyable working environment.

A special word of thanks to Laura Codd (Laura Codd Digital), for her innovative and creative input. Laura's ongoing support and constant positivity is very much appreciated.

Now for those directly involved in the production and publishing of the book thank you :

A huge thanks to **Pat Doran, Enniscorthy**, for his tremendous work on editing the book, copyrighting the book and giving us expert guidance and ideas on how to put the book together. No request was ever too much for Pat.

Pat, thank you for all your work because the book would not have happened without your professional input.

Thank you seems insignificant when it comes to **Barry O'Sullivan Artist** (Enniscorthy) now based in Dublin. Barry did all the artwork for the cover of the book, the graphics inside the book, formatting of the book and much more. This was no easy task considering the novices he was working with. Barry your patience, professionalism and guidance throughout is to be applauded. Barry you played a vital role in getting this book completed. We think your work speaks for itself. Thank you.

Finally to every person we have meet and worked with, socialised with over the years, thank you all for whatever input you had. Everyone you meet in your life has some input; you may never know what that input was so thank you all.

About the Authors

Whitney Career Guidance was founded in 1998 by Seamus Whitney. Seamus developed his unique model of assessing clients to establish their suitability for various careers. This programme became known as the Whitney Career Guidance Model.

In 2010 Seamus was joined by Mary Hickey to further develop and allow greater access to this model. While both parties work independently their professional collaborations has expanded the Whitney Career Guidance Model, making it not only nationally accessible but also internationally accessible. Their client base now spans many countries including Ireland, Australia, Algeria, The Philippines, America, Dubai, and the UK.

Jointly Seamus and Mary hold professional qualifications in many areas including science, management, social sciences, accountancy, training and development, and life coaching to mention just a few They have held multiple roles in many different sectors including, the service industry, the manufacturing industry, the business sector and youth work and social care. Additionally, they have facilitated training workshops with various organisations including the public, private and NGO sectors.

While using the Whitney Career Guidance Model is the foundation of their work, their unique approach and ability to connect with people is what makes this model work. Seamus and Mary have dedicated themselves to empowering countless individuals by helping them uncover and pursue their true career aspirations. Through their support, they have guided many toward achieving their full professional and personal potential.

https://www.whitneycareerguidance.com/

https://maryhickeycareerguidance.com/

Printed in Dunstable, United Kingdom

66699476R00137